This book is not about drama... it's about new ways to inspire students

Myra Barrs | Bob Barton | David Booth

Pembroke Publi

For Dorothy Heathcote
In memoriam

© 2012 Pembroke Publishers
538 Hood Road
Markham, ON, Canada L3R 3K9
www.pembrokepublishers.com

Distributed in the U.S. by Stenhouse Publishers
480 Congress Street
Portland, ME 04101
www.stenhouse.com

We acknowledge the financial support of the Government of Canada through the Book
Publishing Industry Development Program (BPIDP) for our publishing activities.

We acknowledge the assistance of the Government of Ontario through the Ontario
Media Development Corporation's Ontario Book Initiative.

Library and Archives Canada Cataloguing in Publication

Barrs, Myra
    This book is not about drama— : it's about new ways to inspire students / Myra Barrs,
Bob Barton, David Booth.

Includes bibliographical references and index.
Issued also in electronic format.
ISBN 978-1-55138-269-2

    1. Role playing.   2. Drama in education.   3. Language arts (Elementary)—Activity
programs. I. Barton, Robert, 1939–   II. Booth, David III. Title.

PN3171.B36 2012   372.6ʼ044   C2012-903951-9

eBook format ISBN 978-1-55138-843-4

Editor: Kate Revington
Cover Design: John Zehethofer
Typesetting: Jay Tee Graphics Ltd.

Printed and bound in Canada
9 8 7 6 5 4 3 2 1

MIX
Paper from
responsible sources
FSC
www.fsc.org   FSC® C004071

Contents

Introduction: Active and Social Approaches to Literacy

Any class is potentially a close community, a community of learners. Teachers can bring about a sense of community in their classrooms by creating regular opportunities for students to negotiate, collaborate, and share their learning. The cultivation of this kind of community learning spirit can transform the social atmosphere of the class, creating a very positive environment.

The Classroom as a Community of Learners

Many teachers, aware of this potential, always look for ways to provide a focus for the whole class to learn and share together. From shared reading to drama performances to writers' workshops, some of the most successful classroom practices are those that bring students together in social situations to learn from each other and enjoy each other's achievements. Students' confidence grows in situations where they are listened to, involved, and invited to make positive contributions.

Sharing personal stories

This experience is presented in greater detail in *Stories in the Classroom*, by David Booth and Bob Barton.

Here is a case in point. A teacher from London, England, Alan Newland, wrote an article about his class of 10-year-olds. The class had been talking about *The Patchwork Quilt*, a picture book by Valerie Flournoy. To follow up this experience, Newland invited his students to bring in treasured possessions from their earliest memories: old clothes, favorite toys, family photographs. The class responded so enthusiastically that the teacher set aside a whole morning every week for sharing the stories that lay behind the students' treasures. Many of these were highly personal:

> One week a girl brought in a piece of dress material worn by her mother as a maternity smock, accompanied by a letter written by mum recalling the days spent wearing it. A broken old watch had been given to one child's mother as a final parting gift of a dying grandfather.

The atmosphere of trust that had been created in this class enabled the students to share intimate memories that embraced both birth and death.

Over time, the same teacher noticed that, as they told their stories, the students were rapidly becoming highly competent storytellers. He concluded that the students' stories were not simple anecdotes but "appraisals of their experiences." The students were growing in confidence because their experiences were being validated and were becoming significant to themselves and others.

The students' confidence was founded on being taken seriously and being listened to — but also on having opportunities to *practise*. The students were learning from one another how to tell their stories effectively and how to engage their listeners. The class exemplified a close community.

Towards Memorable Learning

All students benefit from learning that is active and social in character. Learning that is participatory, that involves students and engages them, is memorable learning: learning not to be forgotten.

Going inside the story

Here is one instance. In chapter 3 of Henrietta Branford's *Fire, Bed & Bone*, the family in the story remembers when a visiting preacher talked to the villagers about equality and about how the results of their labor were unevenly shared: "The Bible says that God told Adam he must sweat to eat. Do you see the Lord of the Manor, whose harvest you are bringing in just now, sweat for what is laid upon his table? Or do you rather sweat to lay it there?" Students have enacted this scene, through making a still image of it and then bringing the scene to life. Alternatively, they could have extended the story and improvised a scene about what the villagers say to one another when the preacher has left.

Students who do this will have much more active knowledge of the story and of the social history — the Peasants' Revolt — that is central to this book. Rather than discussing the story from a distance, they will have been *inside* the story. This use of *Fire, Bed & Bone* is an example of the way in which active and participatory approaches can support student learning not only in literacy, but right across the curriculum.

Getting out of their seats

In another classroom, this one in a London, United Kingdom, school with high levels of socio-economic deprivation, 10-year-old students read *There's a Boy in the Girls' Bathroom* by Louis Sachar. The teacher found that a sure-fire way to engage her class (which included 12 boys, some of them reluctant students) was to develop dramatic approaches to the novel: these included using dialogue from the novel to create brief play scripts, drawing storyboards of a scene and enacting these, and freeze-framing different scenes before bringing them to life. The students performed their play scripts and scenes for one another — everything they did had an audience.

In interviews after the event, the students were articulate about the aspects of drama that they valued:

- "I like acting because you can move around your body, and you can learn new stories while you do it."
- "You get to stand up and get out of your seats — you don't have to always be sitting and listening to the teacher."

This emphasis on getting out of their seats, on moving around, and of learning with the body as well as the head, was a key element in students' enjoyment of drama. This experience is a long way from "brain gym." In this kind of work, the movement is part of the learning and enriches the learning — it is not a break

Se the Glossary, "Overview of Drama Conventions," for a summary of common drama conventions, including still image.

from it. Students spend far too much time sitting in school, and approaches that enable them to learn with the whole of themselves, to be active and expressive, are likely to prove more effective than approaches where they are glued to their seats.

Collaborating in role

But the ethnically diverse class acting out scenes from the Louis Sachar book also appreciated other aspects of the drama work:

- "You get to work in groups, and when you work in groups you have to organize it together, so you feel like all of you have organized it, not just one person."
- "When we act, we have to organize things, the way we learn, who we get to be, what we have to do. We get to do things which we may never be able to do when we're older."
- "You get to turn into a different person for a few minutes."

These important insights show that the class had appreciated the opportunities for organizing and decision making that this kind of group work had presented them with. They had been expected to behave maturely and to take responsibility, and they had responded to these expectations well. They found working in role to be releasing — they were each enabled to "turn into a different person" and see the world from a different viewpoint.

A Vision for Role-Playing

We recognize the power of working in role. In this book, we offer opportunities for students to interact with the themes, characters, and events in a text through role-playing. They can find themselves inside the lives and actions of the people that fill the stories and texts that they meet in all areas of the curriculum. Part instruction manual, this book provides interactive and artistic strategies and conventions that can enhance co-operative and collaborative meaning-making such as students experience when improvising in role. It thereby provides a way for teachers to recharge the reading and writing activities that they use in their teaching. The relationship between literature and talking in and out of role nurtures and enhances the development of literacy, and supports the deepened meaning-making that can result from working inside and outside a text. Students benefit from exploring this unique relationship.

What role-playing allows students to do

Role-playing, the core of this book, offers students these opportunities:

- to spend time in the shoes of others and conversely, find out more about themselves
- to examine critically the problems and issues that arise in texts, and to seek and rehearse solutions
- to become more aware of cross-cultural relationships, identity, and the power inherent in the words and registers of language
- to find personal voice and learn to listen attentively to each other
- to write in and out of role about the people, events, and reflective meanings that accrue through drama

- to use the information and knowledge gained through reading and research to inform and affect the direction of the drama
- to make plays together, improvising in role and using researched information as they co-create and construct from ideas in texts, and exploring the words of some scripted texts through improvisation and interpretation
- to share with trusted others the plays they have developed in groups through the ensemble process

Working in role helps students generally with their learning. They acquire a technique that enables them to inhabit, in imagination, unfamiliar situations and experiences. There is plenty of evidence that students enjoy this way of learning and that it can engage even reluctant or underachieving students.

PART A

Becoming the Story

In Part A we explore the role played by the imagination in reading, writing, thinking, and learning. We suggest that through entering into the imagined worlds of texts, students can become better readers and writers — more engaged, more skilled and experienced, and more reflective.

The imagination is present in all thinking. Bridge designers have to imagine a bridge before they plan and build it; scientific theories are ways of imagining explanations for phenomena. The trouble with a lot of learning in school is that it assumes that students learn by simply absorbing what they're told. But human beings do not learn passively; they have the capacity to interpret, transform, and build on what they learn. Without the opportunity to interact with ideas, students are likely to switch off.

So, this book presents ways in which school learning, especially in the language arts, can become a more active and engaging experience. In Part A we look at different aspects of learning and at educational theories that support the case for active and experiential learning.

In Chapter 1 we begin with an exploration of what is involved in being a reader — how does a reader enter the world of a text and, temporarily, become part of it? Experienced readers do this automatically: they have become used to inhabiting a text. But inexperienced readers need a lot of book experience and experience of involvement with stories, before they can move into a text in this way. Drama and role play can be seen as *techniques of imagination* — they enable inexperienced readers to be part of a story, to know it from the inside. This is not just a gain in intellectual understanding; it is an affective, or emotional, experience. Once readers have "lived through" a text in this way, they know it differently and can talk and think about it more feelingly, and with more authority.

Drama and role play are ways of taking on different viewpoints and perspectives on a situation — all good thinkers need to be able to do this. Writers, in particular, need the ability to look at their material and take up a stance towards it. In writing the author's viewpoint is crucial. Even quite young students are able to take up a stance by writing in role.

But this book suggests that active role play needs to precede role play on paper. Chapter 2 shows how, through oral rehearsal, imaginative preparation, and full-blown role play, students can access different voices and ways of talking. Teachers who have begun to make use of these techniques of imagination can lead students into exploring new areas of language: areas that they can then draw on in their writing.

Chapter 3 goes more deeply into the question of working in role and how it can enhance students' emotional understanding of characters and situations. In this chapter too, we draw substantially on the seminal work of Dorothy Heathcote who, through her drama teaching, developed detailed ideas about the use of role in learning across the curriculum. She also spelled out the value of teachers taking a role in the drama so as to be able to support students' work in role and influence the progress of the drama from within. Finally, Heathcote's Mantle of the Expert theory has generated a whole educational movement in which teachers have developed their teaching across the curriculum through the systematic use of role. This way of working allows the imagination to have a central part in teaching and learning.

The last chapter in Part A, Chapter 4, considers how teachers can develop understandings of their students' learning in this area by (a) undertaking classroom-based research and (b) recording structured observations of students' work in creative subjects. Here, we also present a model for portfolio assessment in creative learning, based on pioneering work by the Centre for Literacy in Primary Education in London, United Kingdom. The Creative Learning Assessment continuum can be the basis for teachers' assessments in this under-explored aspect of the curriculum. It may also help teachers to reflect on their own practice and evaluate the opportunities they are providing for students to extend their experience of creative learning.

1

Giving the Imagination Play

The Russian psychologist Vygotsky called child play a "leading activity" because he thought it influenced and led young students' wider development. In play, students can go beyond their own limits: "in play it is as though [a child] were a head taller than himself." Through play and pretending, which are early forms of drama, students access modes of behavior and ways of speaking that they don't use in their everyday lives. Vygotsky thought that this kind of pretending was "imagination in action."

Entering a Story Through Role Play

The work described here and in the next section was done as part of the *Reading Differences* project, about teaching world literature in the elementary classroom. The project was carried out by the U.K. Qualifications and Curriculum Authority in collaboration with the Centre for Literacy in Primary Education.

In one Grade 4 classroom, the children studied *The Village That Vanished*, a picture book by Ann Grifalconi, which tells how the members of a West African village outwit the slavers who are scouring the area. The story turns on a formal debate where one of the women, Njemile, convinces her neighbors that their best chance of survival is to dismantle their huts and move away. Although the situation was utterly foreign to them, the students were able to enter the story imaginatively by bringing the text to life.

The students re-enacted the villagers' formal debate, which the teacher described to them as "a kind of organized argument." She gave them 15 minutes in groups to prepare their arguments and then brought them together. Here is part of the transcript:

> **Njemile:** Do you really want to die before you've lived? I think not. We must take the huts apart — we can escape across the river. If we don't go, there's no future for us here — we shall all be taken.
> **A woman:** I'm leaving because the children need to be protected. We can always come back here. If we stay, the slavers will kills us with their long guns.
> **An elder:** I refuse to move. We need to stand up to the slavers. They would get our crops.
> **Child:** We were brought up here. How can we go? I'm scared to leave. I can't cross the river.
> **Chimwala:** I am like a stone. I'll stay. The crocodile doesn't eat the withered snake . . .

As this excerpt indicates, the children took on the language of the book and, through their role play *became* the story, coming to know it in a deeper way.

The strong oral emphasis in this work particularly suited some students who found reading and writing difficult. The teacher commented: "Drama and debate have been the most effective activities. They gained such a lot from thinking about the characters and putting themselves in their positions." Students eagerly took part in the plenary discussions of the book, and some wrote readily in response to the text despite usually being reluctant writers. "It's helped their writing too," the teacher said. "New words and phrases keep coming out."

Interacting with a Literary Text

Louise Rosenblatt, the American educationalist and critic, founded reader response theory, the study of how readers read and what they bring to their reading. Rosenblatt emphasized that the text on the printed page should always be seen as a potential — only in the dynamic to-and-fro between reader and text is the work of art created. But Rosenblatt also felt strongly that students need to be "led to think" about the different social and cultural patterns that they find in books. In *Literature as Exploration*, she wrote: "Through literature we are constantly coming into contact with cultural patterns of the past or of other societies."

Although Rosenblatt believed in the value of exploring the social and cultural aspects of texts, she saw literary works of art as "existing in unique personal experiences." She always insisted on the primacy of the reader's aesthetic experience and on the need to focus on literary response in reading a literary text. Fundamental to her approach to literature is the *quality* of what students are offered in the classroom. She considered that certain texts were more likely to produce thoughtful aesthetic responses in a reader because they had "more potentiality for qualitative response." Whatever their sources and origins, these kinds of texts need to be at the heart of a teaching program.

Case study: *Eye of the Wolf* as a text likely to produce thoughtful responses

Eye of the Wolf by Daniel Pennac is a short, but challenging novel about a boy named Africa, who comes from Africa, and a wolf named Blue Wolf, who comes from Alaska. It raises major questions about life in the places that the two main characters come from, and about the way that humans are destroying wild parts of the world.

Although the book has a single narrator, it shifts the *viewpoint* from which the story is told more than once, while the *setting* moves from the zoo to Alaska, and then on to North Africa and the African rain forest. Pennac's skill is to deal with a wide geopolitical canvas and a complex narrative structure in a short space. Not many novels written in English seem to offer readers of this age this kind of engagement with a wider contemporary world.

The teacher of one Grade 6 class commented: "I don't think many English books deal with these issues. They go for easier ingredients — a bit of mystery, a bit of magic. This is more mature. We underestimate what students can discuss."

The class listened to some of the story read aloud and read other chapters independently in groups, recording their discussion as it went along as notes, as lists, or in graphic form. They were used to listening to each other, responding to each other's ideas, and exploring their responses. One group discussed their impressions of the family of wolves that Blue Wolf comes from in this fashion:

A: So what do we think about the way the wolves see humans?
B: The only humans they know are hunters and the only thing the hunters want to do is to kill them.

C: The red cubs haven't actually seen a human, they're still immature, they want to play more, they want freedom. They might think they're never going to get caught.

D: We're hearing a bit more about Grey Cousin now, he's coming into the story more, he's saying more.

E: He says that's what humans are, but not all humans have guns — they think *all* humans are hunters . . .

F: Grey Cousin's just the watch, he's not the wisest . . .

G: Wise isn't smart, it's knowing about life and everything. I think Blue Wolf is the wisest.

The group felt that their discussion had deepened their response to the book. They were beginning to appreciate the book's shape, saying: "It's all beginning to hang together."

Their teacher said: "They enjoy discussion, and we've been spending time discussing how to have a discussion. So this work was very well suited to them." The class's experience was apparent in their ability to listen to and build on each other's points, float tentative ideas, and keep track of their overall argument. The teacher used a whiteboard to record student responses; this provided a complete record of the class's discussions and allowed her to review with the students how their thinking was changing and how the story was developing. She found them responsive to the book's sophisticated narrative style, calling them "good readers . . . aware of what the writer's doing."

Thinking Together About a Book

This kind of talk is vital for readers' development: through talking about books they come to see into them more deeply and to feel their way into the experiences of the characters. Talking about individual passages in books can draw out what readers think is going on, or draw attention to the way a particular character talks or behaves, or to what the writer is doing. Group talk enables several people to share their responses and reactions, and benefit from each other's insights. That's why it has become quite common for groups of adults to meet in reading groups; doing so enables them to derive more from their reading.

Tell me . . .

At best, these kinds of conversations around texts can help students to *think together* about a book. Reflective group talk needs to be carefully encouraged and managed by the teacher, so that all students have the space to think and to share even quite tentative ideas and feelings. Aidan Chambers has provided a very thorough description of how such talk can be fostered and developed in *Tell Me: Children, Reading and Talk*. The title contains one key feature of this approach: rather than asking direct questions, the teacher invites children to share their ideas:

- Tell me what you liked about this book [this chapter]. (likes)
- Was there anything you didn't like in it? Tell me about it. (dislikes)
- Tell me whether there was anything that puzzled you in this book. (puzzles)
- I wonder if you saw any patterns in the book — any connections? Can you tell me about them? (patterns)

When children are asked direct questions, they sometimes feel put on the spot, and they may try to guess what the teacher wants them to say. But there are no right or wrong answers to "tell me" questions, so discussion is less competitive and more reflective. The four areas touched on in the "tell me" questions — likes, dislikes, puzzles, and patterns — are offered as a way of structuring talk around books; they provide an open framework for the discussion. Gradually, the group builds up a fuller shared picture of what members have been reading.

Case study: "The Sea Woman" as a basis for discussion and role play

Developing as a reader involves an ability to engage emotionally with the story. The sense of being inside the story, involved with the characters and their dilemmas, keeps readers reading.

In the following piece of transcript, three children from a Grade 5 class are discussing the story "The Sea Woman" with their teacher. They are imagining themselves in the situation of the Sea Woman's children, who lost their mother when she found her hidden sealskin and returned to the sea:

> **T:** I would feel devastated if I was one of the children. To find out that your dad is trapping your mom.
> **A:** I would be experiencing the leaving.
> **Teacher P:** Yes, you would be suffering that loss yourself.
> **A:** I would feel worse and worse. It's better to have both your parents.
> **N:** They might not want her to come back. She might lie again. They don't trust her.

How does the teacher's language influence the language that students use when they talk together? Here, the teacher affirms what child A says, which encourages child A to explore his feelings more deeply. These young students are approaching the emotional situation of this story in a mature way, and the teacher helps them to talk about the psychology of the situation. Talk can encourage students to explore complex ideas and feelings, both in literature and in life.

Drama and role play, another way of experiencing emotional identification with the text, often lead to the kind of feeling talk that these students are engaging in. Later, the same group of students took part in a role play related to this story: a courtroom drama called "The Seal Wife in Divorce Court." In the piece of transcript that follows, one student is speaking in role *as* the Sea Woman:

> It was wrong to steal someone's freedom like MacCodrum did to me and ruin my life by holding me and imprisoning me by taking my skin. I love him deep down but I hate the fact that he stole my skin and for interfering in my life. I can't forgive MacCodrum for stealing my skin and my freedom which was wrong.

Working in role has helped this girl to get inside a literary situation and become the character in her imagination. Her language here has some of the formality appropriate to the courtroom situation. She makes clear the ambiguity of her feelings, complicated by her continuing love for the fisherman, but she is unequivocal about the wrong that has been done to her by his stealing her skin, imprisoning her, interfering in her life, and taking her freedom. Her speech is a morally powerful statement.

This work was carried out as part of a research project on promoting boys' literacy, the findings of which were published by the Centre for Literacy in Primary Education as *Boys on the Margin*.

"The Sea Woman" by Kevin Crossley-Holland appears in the author's collection of stories called *The Magic Lands*, which is published by Orion.

Trying On, Trying Out

Older students can develop their ability to pretend, to empathize, to *become*, to "think from within" through more formal activities in drama. They are able to imagine, without recourse to physical pretending. Imagining and thinking from within are powerful ways of taking on and understanding experience that is different from our own. American Mildred Taylor, author of *Roll of Thunder, Hear My Cry*, recognized this when she expressed this goal for her writing:

> Since writing my first book . . . it has been my wish to have readers walk in the shoes of the Logan family . . . and to feel what they felt. It has been my wish that by understanding this family and what they endured, there would be further understanding of what millions of families endured, and there would also be a further understanding of why there was a Civil Rights movement, a movement that changed our nation.

Walking in the shoes of others fosters empathy and insight into their lives — it is also what happens in role play. Drama is a key route to this deep kind of learning. It can therefore be seen as a form of both emotional and moral education. And, as we have been establishing, it is also a major way into literacy.

These ideas have significance for students at every stage of education. Role play offers opportunities for students to try on personae, try out behavior, assume ways of speaking, confront imaginary situations, and negotiate the development of these scenarios with their peers. In this sense, play, which is first the preserve of children, never ceases to be a "leading activity," even for grown-up students.

2

Talking Their Way into Writing

When students take part in discussions in role — putting themselves in other people's shoes — they are able to try out ideas and rehearse through talk. This kind of oral rehearsal helps children to put their thoughts into words and to develop them. Oral rehearsal helps children to think, but also acts as a preparation for writing.

Oral Rehearsal as a Halfway House

Oral rehearsal can be seen as a halfway house between thought and writing. The Russian psychologist Vygotsky made the point that when we write, we are *taking thought the furthest distance that it has to travel*. The diagram below is one way of illustrating this.

Thought–Writing Continuum
inner speech ⟶ oral speech ⟶ written speech

Inner speech, or what Vygotsky also called "verbal thought," is the most condensed form of language; *written speech* (or written language) is the most complex and elaborate form of language — it has a very different grammar from oral speech. Moving thought into written language thus involves a form of translation, a translation from the *extremely condensed* expression of a thought-idea into the *elaborated* expression of it in writing. And that, says Vygotsky, is why writing is difficult.

But the diagram also makes clear that there is an intermediate stage in this process — *oral speech,* or talk. Many of us have recourse to talk when we're trying to think out what to write. Often, we find somebody to talk to about what we're trying to say, and once having rehearsed our meanings orally, we find we can write them down. The poet Coleridge, when he got stuck with his writing, *talked* his books — he was someone who could talk better than he wrote. He always needed someone to be there to listen to his talk and transcribe what he was saying.

So talk provides us with the pedagogical way into the thinking–writing process: *students can be encouraged to talk their meanings before they write them down.* That realization has led us to all kinds of classroom practices, such as writing conferences, scribing, shared writing, paired writing, response partners, and editing partners — all potentially excellent ways of helping students to move thoughts into written language.

From discussion into role play

Oral rehearsal can happen through discussion, with children putting forward their views about a particular situation. For instance, they might be discussing how to convince their own mother if, like Mrs. Sparrow in Philippa Pearce's *The Battle of Bubble and Squeak*, she was completely opposed to them keeping a pet. What would be the most convincing arguments in this situation?

A discussion on a topic like this would move naturally into role play, a more developed form of oral rehearsal. Here, children could get inside the story world and explore ideas and feelings from there. Having to speak as a particular character means taking on that character's point of view and voice. When children do so, they are helped to move into areas of language that they might not otherwise be so able to access.

Imaginative Preparation

"Unpacking the Story," on pages 83 to 86, provides an example of students moving from enacting a poem, "What Has Happened to Lulu?" by Charles Causley, to writing in role with intensity and commitment.

Oral rehearsal is a wonderful way of preparing for writing. Through discussion and role play, childen will begin to build up a rich picture of the world of the story. They will often have a mental picture of the story setting — for instance, they may be able to describe the house the characters live in — and this description can be refined through discussion. Perhaps they will have developed ideas about what the characters look like, how they dress, and how they speak. Role play encourages this kind of visualization and imagining. When children begin to write, they will be able to draw on their own mental pictures. This kind of imaginative preparation can make writing much less daunting.

Many teachers have found that oral rehearsal is a positive way of supporting children with writing. "Role play is good," says one, because it gives them a chance to rehearse the language before they start writing." "Oral rehearsal needs to happen not only as individuals but in a group," says another. "When they're interacting and talking to each other, they are much more able to come out with their ideas and imagine what to say."

Language as the heart of the drama process

The account of David's work with the Grade 4 class is presented in detail in *Story Drama*, published by Pembroke.

David Booth was working with a Grade 4 class identified as having behavioral problems. Using Jane Yolen's *Children of the Wolf* as stimulus, he and the class began with a discussion of books and films they had seen concerning children raised by creatures of the jungle or forest — Tarzan, Mowgli, wolf children. David presented the students with the problem to be solved through drama:

> We are a group of scientists who have been awarded the contract for developing a program for humanizing a twelve year old boy, discovered living in a jungle, raised by wolves. In four years it is our job to create a civilized sixteen-year-old man who will have a chance at a normal life. The first step for our group is to create a set of priorities concerning the training of the wolf boy.

The children worked in groups as scientists to construct a program and confront the problems involved in changing the wolf boy's behavior and values. Different groups developed strategies for working on the wolf boy's language, his clothing, his food and eating, his social habits, and his emotional needs. They presented their ideas to the whole class, who offered comments and suggestions.

David then raised the stakes and telescoped time by announcing that one year had passed and that each group had to reveal the progress it had made. He reported:

The language of the children dramatically changed as the groups presented their findings. They took their roles as scientists very seriously, using their notes from their clipboards as the basis for their discussion. Their body language, choice of words, sense of audience, strength in role became much more complex. They seemed to think of themselves as authorities as their commitment to the drama grew.

All of this, David notes, was accomplished through language. Nobody saw the wolf boy, and nobody played him in role; instead, "the children talked about him and created him in his absence." This was a powerful piece of drama in which talk in role was the medium for learning. And what important learning! Through the language of role play, these children, who were considered to have behavioral difficulties, had become scientists with a real perspective on how human behavior can be changed and developed, how a wild boy can be socialized. As David says, "Language is the heart of the drama process and the means through which the drama is realized."

The Transformative Power of Role Play

Once students enter imaginatively into a dramatic situation, or a role, they are often able to access other ways of talking. Putting oneself in somebody else's shoes can be transformative; it can enable someone to get closer to that person's thinking and way of using language. The implications for the teaching of language and literacy are clear: children who have begun to think from within, and who have learned to empathize with characters very different from their own, are able to take on the language of these characters too. In the process, they broaden their own linguistic range.

This insight applies just as much to written language as to oral language. Once a student has been able to enter into the thoughts and feelings of a character through role play or drama, it is much easier for the student to put thoughts on paper or screen in the voice appropriate to the character. The transformative power of role helps children to take on other voices and enter other linguistic worlds.

How to release the power to write

This work took place as part of a project on literature and writing development, which will be explored in more depth below.

One example of how role play can release the power to write comes from an account by a teacher who took part in a drama workshop based on Kevin Crossley-Holland's telling of "The Wildman." This old story is about a wild merman who is captured by fishers and incarcerated in the village dungeon at Orford, on the east coast of England.

"This workshop was conducted by a well-known drama teacher. First of all, the group became members of a production team for a TV documentary program about the story; we were told that there was a rumor going round about the presence of a merman in the sea off Orford, and we had been commissioned to film the events there — we each had our own roles in the team and we discussed the problems of filming in this situation, and how we would work together.

"Next, we re-created the story itself through a succession of still images; we worked in small groups and each group took a scene from the story to make into a still photo, or freeze-frame, using mime. These still 'photos' showed such scenes as the precise moment when the Wildman was caught in the fishermen's nets, and the ugly scene of the villagers taunting the Wildman before shutting him in the dungeon.

"Finally, the workshop leader, in role as a visiting bishop, asked us to imagine that we were all villagers who had been called to a meeting in the village inn. Upstairs the bishop would be taking evidence about the capture and ill treatment of the Wildman. Choosing our own roles as villagers, we had to write our personal accounts of what had happened, in preparation for giving evidence. We were sternly warned to tell 'the truth and nothing but the truth.'

"As soon as we were given the cue to start writing, we began to write almost immediately. It was amazing how readily the writing came — we knew exactly who we were and what viewpoint we were writing from, we knew the whole story, we had lived through the events, and we were truly inside them. Many of us had taken part in the merman-baiting and were now ashamed of what we had done; our private doubts spilled onto the paper. I found myself writing confidently and fast in the role I had chosen, that of the village midwife. It made me see how very important it is to spend time on preparation — imaginative preparation — for writing."

How to write to a king

Young children who have taken part in a whole-class drama, such as one based on Lloyd Alexander's *The King's Fountain*, are also empowered by the experience of writing from within a known situation and a known role. David Booth has described *The King's Fountain* as "one of my most important sources for drama teaching." The story about a greedy king who wants to build a fountain which will take the water away from a poor village is full of complexities and dilemmas, all of which can be explored through drama.

David describes how, after taking part in a whole-class drama based on the story, a Grade 4 class went on to write letters petitioning the king. These appeals were written in fine calligraphy with illuminated letters, and they used language appropriate for addressing a king. One example:

Dear King

Your town, which soon faces destruction, is asking you if you would stop the building of the fountain. If you won't stop, we have some reasons why you should. Most of the people are too old to walk twenty miles to get water that their families need. The children are too young to get the water because they don't know their way to the east and the wild animals might kill them. The merchants want more for getting the water and want the poor to pay for that water . . . .

Children who take on grown-up roles in a drama can often take on grown-up language too. They are, of course, familiar with adult language both from real life and from television, but often only in a make-believe context do they gain the opportunity to use it and to reveal their considerable linguistic knowledge. Just as Vygotsky describes children who take part in make-believe play as being "a head taller," so too are children who take part in a drama which puts them into adult roles and challenging situations.

Writing in Role with Authority

A full account of the research described here can be found in *The Reader in the Writer* by Myra Barrs and Valerie Cork, published by the U.K.'s Centre for Literacy in Primary Education.

In a research project designed to look at the influence of children's reading of literature on their writing, one finding was that drama can provide a strikingly immediate route into the world of a text. All of the six Grade 4 classes involved in the project took part in a drama workshop *before* their reading of a folk tale, Kevin Crossley-Holland's *The Green Children*. In most classrooms, this drama work led to writing that was thoroughly imagined and qualitatively different from the writing that the students had done before. Enabling the children to "live through" part of the fiction before encountering it meant that they were thoroughly engaged in the story from the inside. The drama workshop was a watershed in the project; the drama experience had triggered an affective, or emotional, response and led to a strong commitment to the work. As noted in *The Reader in the Writer,* "The words of the text had been brought within their realm of knowing and a bridge built between the world of the text and the way a writer makes a world from language and imagination" (p. 224).

The roles the children had taken in the drama encouraged them to write in different voices and from different viewpoints; however, their subsequent reading of Kevin Crossley-Holland's text also greatly influenced their writing and shaped their style. The combination of the insights gained through drama and the rhythms and patterns of Crossley-Holland's prose moved the children's writing into new territory.

Writing development through role play

For instance, Grace, one child who featured in the research, had been a fluent writer at the beginning of the year, but her stories were generally straightforward, conversational narratives with school settings. They moved quickly with a strong onward momentum. She rarely paused the narrative to explore the world and setting of the story, or to reveal characters' feelings or thoughts. Her first story of the school year began:

> I was sitting down in class I had finished all my work I was reading a very boring book so instead I looked out of the window like most children in the class do. Anyway I was chewing my pencil at the same time. Then suddenly a little voice came from my pencil saying, "Hey how would you like it if someone was writing with your feet and chewing your hair off?" "Who said that" I shouted look down. Then I saw my pencil talking I screamed the whole class looked at me.

Yet five months later, in her Green Children writing, Grace slows the pace, and her narration has more pauses and more atmosphere — she is consciously creating the world of the story:

> The green creature came closer, and closer, I noticed it was a child. But before I could say anything else, the green child ran away. I couldn't see her anymore, she was camouflaged with the olive green grass and the silky green leaves, that was the last time I saw her. I was confused. Most people thought it was their imagination but I knew it was real. I'll never forget that moment and I'll always wonder what she was and where she was from.

In this passage, Grace writes with more inwardness — in role as an adult villager, she describes her state of mind, her feelings, her thoughts, and her wonderings. Her sentences are shorter and more dramatic. Although the rest of her text often echoed Kevin Crossley-Holland's original, the above passage is completely original; there are no sources for it in the Crossley-Holland story. In the course of the project, the research team that analyzed the samples of her writing judged that Grace's work developed greatly. By the end of the project, her narrative voice and her sense of the reader were both much stronger, and she was more used to exploring characters' feelings and thoughts in her writing, giving an overall impression of a more mature writer with greater control over her narratives.

Drama on paper

One of the project's conclusions was that writing in role — writing in first person, but not as themselves — had extended the children's range as writers. It had produced quite different kinds of texts from their normal first-person writing. This experience helped the children to assume different voices and to enter areas of language that they did not normally use. It helped them to try out other viewpoints and to write from alternative perspectives. It also led them to write from "inside" the story more, to identify with very different characters, and to explore the mental states of these characters more fully.

Writing in role might be regarded as "drama on paper." Beyond this idea, one thing that became clear through this research was that the drama workshop teachers and children had experienced served as powerful preparation for writing around texts. The drama had helped them to open up the texts and explore fictional worlds, both through role play and through writing in role. In the next chapter, we explore further evidence of what happens when teachers use work in role to bring texts to life.

3

Understanding Character Through Role Play

What we might call "imagining in the body" is always a key part of work in drama. It is often very important for people trying to get inside a dramatic situation to physically place themselves in it. They can do so by using movement, or even just gesture and body language (as in tableaux), to express an interpretation of the situation.

Use of a Simple Technique: Still Image

The research described here can be found in "Engaging Critical Reader Response to Literature Through Process Drama," a *Reading Online* article by Margery Hertzberg. This project was carried out in a suburban school in Sydney, Australia. Excerpts are quoted with the author's explicit permission.

Even a simple dramatic technique can bring a text to life for students. In this classroom-based research, an Australian drama teacher, Margery Hertzberg, worked with a Grade 5 class teacher to explore a text, *Onion Tears*, about a Vietnamese immigrant student in an Australian classroom. Other students in the class are intrigued by the immigrant's Vietnamese name and want to know what it means. Their remarks are teasing, jeering, and bullying.

Using a technique she calls "still image," Hertzberg asked the class, in groups of four, to make tableaux of this scene from the story. They had to use space, gesture, body language, and facial expression to communicate what was going on. They then showed their still images to the rest of the class and discussed them. These discussions demonstrated how much they had gained from using mime and gesture to express the tension of the scene. Hertzberg notes:

> It was clear to students that this scene was a portrayal of emotional abuse, but through assuming roles and then planning the still image, they were able to explore the physical nuances that contribute to the development of both the characters and the themes. Students not only analyzed the author's meanings, but they brought to the text their own voices and experiences. Using drama and, by implication, paralinguistics as a means for interpreting a point of tension, helped because students were able to "represent more than they would be able to communicate through words alone."

The following comments come from various audio and video interviews of class members. They are representative of the class's view about still image:

Bill: Yeah, acting out that character, like, it makes you feel like you are them. You know more about the character.
Jake: You can understand it, 'cause you're the one who's, like, in the shoes sort of. And you're the one who's doing it, so you understand it.
Kate: You can use as much body and facial expression as you want to, so people watching us can see who our characters are . . . By the expression

on your face and the way you're sitting and moving around, people can tell how you feel.

John: Because it, like, helps you in reading, writing. Helps you understand heaps of stuff that you never understand, as well as if you don't do drama. Usually, like, when you read books, you don't understand it but when you're doing drama you understand why they're feeling and how.

These comments are hesitant but revealing; they show students working their way towards a realization of how this simple drama technique has helped them to get inside the text, and how it has helped them to empathize with and even become another person from a very different background. They have literally put themselves in someone else's place. The power of this mode of learning through the body is convincingly demonstrated by this small-scale piece of research.

Thinking from Within

The National Writing Project is a long-standing American initiative whereby teacher-leaders share effective, well-researched practices with interested educators across the country. In a conversation-interview for this professional development forum, Jim Lobdell, of University of California, Berkeley, spoke with Courtney Cazden, of Harvard University, about how drama could be used in the writing program.

The full conversation was published in *The Quarterly of the National Writing Project* 15, no. 3.

Lobdell: It seems to me that one of the important things drama could do . . . would be to help the students find ways to work from "inside the dilemma," as Dorothy Heathcote phrases it.

Cazden: To think from within.

Lobdell: Precisely. Getting into the character — whether it's a fictional character in a play or in a short story that students write, or a real character in a real-life situation or a historical situation — involves getting inside that character's thoughts and feelings.

Cazden: They can do it mentally.

Lobdell went on to describe working with teachers of American literature and their Grade 11 students on a Faulkner short story, "Wash." The goal was to look at multiple perspectives. Lobdell and the teachers divided the students into three groups representing the major groups in the society portrayed by Faulkner: the aristocratic whites, the poor whites, and the blacks. They then worked on staging an inquest based on the incidents in the story. Lobdell reported:

At first it was just dismal, like pulling teeth, until we got a number of students in each group to take on the roles of individual characters, such as Ku Klux Klan members and former slaves who were now free. Then, because their roles were more clearly defined we were able to have people — students — give testimony on the stand who were thinking from inside the heads of the characters, all imaginatively living in that context at that time. . . . If the bell had not rung, and if students had written at that moment, they would have written fluently for the entire time, because they had so much to say. . . . My experience is that after students have done this sort of activity a number of times, they can often write imaginatively without actually doing the acting prior to writing.

The ability to think from within the heads of others is a key aspect of mental development. As indicated earlier, Vygotsky argued that imagination forms a part of all thinking — so, for example, scientists who hypothesize are engaging in *imaginative* activity. Drama is a way of putting students into different situations and roles so that imaginatively, they confront different challenges. Learners who have experienced this kind of thinking from within may be able to internalize it and draw on these internal resources in thinking and writing.

The Use of Role: The Ideas of Dorothy Heathcote

It would be difficult to discuss any issues relating to educational drama or the use of role without acknowledging the great influence that Dorothy Heathcote's work has had on drama teaching, but also on the use of role in learning. Heathcote's work has foregrounded three essential tools in teaching through drama: (1) the use of role; (2) the importance of teacher-in-role, that is, the teacher taking a role in the drama; and (3) the value of students taking on roles as experts, assuming the Mantle of the Expert.

1. The use of role

See *Dorothy Heathcote: Collected Writings on Education and Drama*, edited by Liz Johnson and Cecily O'Neill, for more detail on Heathcote's approach.

In Heathcote's approach, students are never asked to act a part; rather, they are asked to assume a role in the situation being developed through the drama. Theatre skills are not required; what is required is the students' belief in their roles and the ability to place themselves in the shoes of another. Because this kind of drama is low threat, students are never put under too much pressure — the whole group can become involved, at whatever level they feel capable of participating. Heathcote said:

> I work slowly in the beginning. I do not move forward until the class is committed to the work. . . . I do not expect classes to like drama automatically. I guarantee that I will do nothing to make them feel foolish but neither will I allow them to get off the hook. (p. 102)

Heathcote focused on creating imagined situations with the class, with much of the initial work taken up with building belief — establishing the central dramatic situation. In one instance, a class chose to create a drama about a ship at sea. Heathcote asked them how the ship was powered, whether it was modern or old-fashioned, and whether the drama would take place in modern or olden times. She gradually established the world of the drama. She then asked the class what jobs they would do and listed each student's real name with his or her responsibility aboard the sailing ship — lookout, cabin boy, second mate, sail maker, carpenter, and so on. Their roles decided, the crew members went about their jobs, getting the ship ready to go to sea, and in the process, establishing their roles more clearly. As the ship set sail, they met increasing challenges — for instance, hoisting 54 sails. But in the middle of this activity, they were also faced with a serious crisis — the captain was suddenly discovered dead on the deck. Heathcote observed:

Placing yourself in the shoes of another suddenly brings you into time-pressure which is a feature of dramatic activity; the need to do something about it now. . . . People in drama are now, here, and under pressure to act in situations. That is the tension of drama. (p. 129)

2. The teacher-in-role

In the sailing ship drama, Heathcote initially took on the role of a harsh first mate in order to direct the dramatic activity from within the drama. She said, "The teacher must be prepared to enter the students' world once they begin to work in the medium" (Johnson and O'Neill, p. 47). By entering that world, Heathcote helped to give validity and importance to their ideas and helped them to develop those ideas from *within the drama*. She could also lead and control the drama, feeding in information and developing the dramatic situation. The teacher-in-role could be a person with a problem, asking the class for advice, as when Heathcote involved a class of six- and seven-year-olds in helping her to work out what kind of house she would need for 19 orphans. Or the teacher-in-role could adopt a more dominant role — which sometimes unites the class against the teacher, as happened in the sailing ship drama.

An effective feature of Heathcote's teacher-in-role work is that it enabled her to stop the drama periodically and ask the class to reflect on what had happened so far. Doing this enables a class to stand back and consider the dramatic situation they have all been part of and to make choices about how it should develop. Heathcote would ask a question like "How are you feeling now?" An observer reported:

> She often goes round from person to person asking what each has been feeling. As these inner responses are shared new depths are sounded. For example, one time when a group was doing a drama about a voyage into outer space, a girl who had been in role as one of the astronaut's wives told the group that she had trouble getting through her usual morning routines. . . . "I suddenly felt sad and thought what if he didn't come back? . . . We'd miss him terrible. Our space here would be awful — like that out there." (p. 78)

The teacher's ability to switch between in-role and out-of-role work, and therefore, to build in reflection through out-of-role discussions, introduces a new dimension to the drama. And it makes different linguistic demands on the students, who, through this switching, are led to be more evaluative and sometimes more analytical about the work in role.

3. The Mantle of the Expert

Many of the dramas Heathcote created with students placed them in specialist roles, for example, the seamen on the sailing ship or members of a mountain rescue team. Generally, in the course of such a drama, the students learn more about their roles, their field of expertise, and the specialist work they do. For instance, some of the dramas that Heathcote directed featured archeological investigations. Students became expert archeologists on a dig, carefully brushing the earth from a specimen of pottery, or specialist curators in a museum, categorizing and labelling archeological finds. In both these cases, the nature of the work foregrounds the importance of meticulous care and accuracy, and careful hypothetical thinking — paying attention to the evidence.

This kind of drama enabled Heathcote to lead a class into different kinds of worlds and to explore many different branches of knowledge. For this reason, Mantle of the Expert approaches have increasingly been adopted: they offer imaginative and accessible ways into topics right across the school curriculum. In "Role Play: How Teaching Make-Believe Gets Real Results," a journalist who visited Bealings primary school in Norfolk, England, explains how role play "allows the school to create a whole world of learning environments."

"Role Play: How Teaching Make-Believe Gets Real Results" was written by Brian Hicks. The article appeared in *The Independent*, a U.K. newspaper, on December 1, 2007. Excerpt published with permission.

Over the past few years, Bealings students have run a bear sanctuary, an oil rig, a travel agency, a trucking company, a demolition firm, and many other ventures — all within the walls of the school. These imaginary enterprises often have a commercial side, with the teachers acting as clients providing commissions, which have to be costed and documented and carried out by the students. The genius of this school has been to adopt the role play technique to deliver large chunks of the national curriculum. Each scenario has to be meticulously planned so that key aspects of literacy, numeracy, science, geography and history emerge at the right time, and are mastered. This term, for example, Years 3 and 4 have been working together as the management team of a thriving container port — Bealixstowe. It doesn't exist, but to the students, while they're in role, it is as real as the similarly named port a few miles up the A12. They have already covered a great deal of maths — the volumes of containers, the numbers that can be stacked in the terminal — and geography, in the origins and destinations of ships and their cargoes.

But today, their teacher, Kelly King, in the role of a concerned member of the public, presents them with an ethical dilemma — a tip-off that some contraband has arrived from Venezuela. The students have to decide what to do, so they meet, discuss the problem, and act — searching the containers, eventually (after more debate) breaking into the suspect box and finding fashion items which, according to their labels, are made from the finest Orinoco crocodile skin. A child is nominated to research the material on Google (tick ICT skills) and their worst fears are confirmed— it's the skin of an endangered species. They meet again and vote on whether to call the police, at which point the teacher says, "Right! Leave the mantle there. But first, help me put the tables back."

Students Standing "a Head Taller"

Students taking part in dramas such as the news article describes are working in very different linguistic registers from those they normally use. Those engaged in Mantle of the Expert approaches use language in more sophisticated ways than usual. Often taking on adult roles, roles that involve expertise, they are being led to use language in new ways: to frame hypotheses, to assess evidence, to give expert opinions, and to propose solutions to problems.

The changes in students taking part in these kinds of dramas are tangible. As Vygotsky put it, they often seem "a head taller"; they can try on adult roles and use their knowledge of how issues are addressed in the wider world beyond school. And the rich contextual knowledge they are building up of the worlds they are creating through the drama often enables them to speak — and even write — with confidence and authority. For instance, one boy — normally a reluctant writer — was involved in a drama about a diving company specializing in undersea rescue. He was moved to write a whole page for the company records about when he had to dive through sharks, puffa fish, and an oil slick to reach a stricken oil tanker.

When students engage in drama as part of the literacy curriculum, they gain opportunities to use

- *speculative and hypothetical* language (what might happen)
- *interactive, co-operative* language during the planning stages (what is going to happen)
- *imaginative, expressive* language during the drama-in-role phase (what is happening)
- *reflective, evaluative* language at the completion of the drama (what has happened, why did it happen, what could have happened)

Working in role can be a transformative experience for students and for teachers. It provides them with a remarkable tool for exploring and understanding different situations and areas of knowledge. As they enter these other worlds, the challenges they face lead to changes in their ways of thinking and their ways of using language.

4

Observing Students Inside the Learning

In this book, we include many examples of young people at work in drama, providing transcripts, recounts of lessons, and summaries of our experiences with students. A key reason for doing so is to help all teachers recognize the importance of closely observing their students. By observing students inside the learning, teachers can build on their ideas and help them develop their work. As they observe students' learning, they are taking the perspective of action researchers — studying a classroom situation in order to change their own practice. They are also gathering evidence that will eventually help them to document and evaluate or assess students' progress.

Taking Action Research Initiatives

When teachers undertake action research, they observe their students, making notes of how they see students' work develop. By so doing, they can keep track of the effects of new approaches to literacy teaching. This kind of classroom-based research enables teachers to see the difference that their teaching is making. It also provides evidence for others of the value of active and creative practices.

Most action research involves case study — observing particular students, tracking their learning in detail, and reflecting on the implications. One advantage of this kind of observation is that it helps the teacher to teach particular learners — and ultimately learners in general — more effectively. But teachers' case studies also enable a wider audience to see into the process of learning, and to share the realization of how learners can change and develop.

Two examples of specific action research projects follow.

Project: The effect of storytelling on writing

One English action research project, Animating Literacy, brought together a group of teachers who aimed to document the impact of arts partnerships on literacy learning. The project involved the teachers in working with arts partners in the classroom throughout a school year. The teachers decided on research questions for their individual class projects and were given regular opportunities to meet together, reflect on their projects, discuss any issues that arose, and share their research findings, subsequently published by the Centre for Literacy in Primary Education as *Animating Literacy*.

One teacher, Anne, wanted to see how regular involvement in oral storytelling would affect students' writing. She worked with a professional storyteller to develop students' storytelling skills and help them to explore story worlds. She began this work with a Grade 2 class, and in the subsequent year continued it with a Grade 5 class.

In the Grade 2 class, Anne noted:

All the students developed speaking and listening skills. They learnt to hear the structure of story and patterns of literary language. They had time to reflect and rehearse stories in their minds before telling them to others. . . .

Storytelling is a social and shared experience and during the course of the year the shared stories, opportunities to perform, and peer support formed strong bonds between the students. In terms of writing, the whole experience of storytelling gave students an inner voice to express and motivation to express it.

One student in this class stated: "Before Jan [the storyteller] came I couldn't read or write or tell stories. Now I can read and write and tell stories." The storyteller had not, in fact, done *any* teaching of reading or writing in this project — but storytelling had changed these students' views of themselves. As Anne put it: "They became masters of words and language instead of feeling defeated by them . . . we all started to feel like experts in the art of storytelling."

Project: The links between artistic activities and literacy

Other teacher-researchers have found that the experience of observing students and documenting their learning gives them access to powerful evidence of the relationships between students' involvement in artistic activities and their literacy development.

In a project on the assessment of creative learning, Becky, an English teacher-researcher, worked with both a visual artist and a visiting actor during the school year. She noted the effects on her own learning as well as that of the students:

The involvement of the arts partners impacted on my professional development, I was learning alongside the children. As I developed my skills and knowledge, I was more empowered and informed to teach and assess the students' subject knowledge and understanding. My vocabulary and explanations became more specific and explicit; I was using the technical language of the subject with greater confidence and understanding.

Gradually the students' talk also became more skilled: they took on the patterns of talk appropriate to the artistic context, began to use subject-specific language and expressed their thinking more clearly and with greater focus:

"I used the sculpting tools, cutting, scooping, smoothing my statue. Can you see the fibres in the clay? I think it'll dry quickly as it's warm in here. But if it dries too quickly — it might crack." — Lamarna (age 8 years)

Becky was interested in the impact that involvement in creative activities could have on students' literacy, specifically their writing. So, with her second arts partner, the actor, she observed the way in which drama — especially mime, a very physical form of drama — influenced students' ability to imagine on paper:

As the teacher, I had to identify what experience the students needed and then negotiate this with each artist. For example, the students needed to develop their writing, so we planned an improvisation project to support this. I wanted the students to explore their own ideas through drama before writing, as well as to develop their understanding and skills within this creative form.

Through mime, the visiting actor helped students to imagine the experience of caged zoo animals, to become the animals and to improvise a story of escape. Initially the actor concentrated on demonstrating how a tiger, gorilla, and penguin moved in a cage. The students' miming skills rapidly developed because they were more informed and supported.

The sessions were videoed, and the differences between the first and third sessions were fascinating, from a riot of noise and movement to cathedral-like silence as students watched each other move with poise and expression. Following this, students' writing became far more expansive and vivid. It was drama that supported them in writing more powerfully and convincingly, from inside the text.

Getting inside the text, living through the story, and thinking from inside the characters' heads — all of these are descriptions of what can happen when students are helped, through drama, to empathize with a fictional situation, identify with its characters, and experience the action from inside. Becky's account in this passage of how the students' work in mime changed radically — how they became more skillful and expressive in their movements — is powerfully expressed in her description of the "cathedral-like silence" that fell as they watched one another move.

These examples of students learning to master particular artistic skills, and of a teacher becoming more expert in her observation of their creative progress, indicate how much teachers can benefit from action research. Both examples of Becky's work with arts partners in the classroom show how much knowledge and understanding she gained from her detailed observations and from recording individual students' learning.

The value of structured observation

These kinds of observations and records are powerful evidence to support teachers' later assessments of students' progress. The evidence of progress they provide is much more valuable than any one-off assessment; this kind of evidence records students' strengths and also points to the areas where they need support. Although the assessment of creative work is difficult, structured observation makes it achievable.

Assessing Creative Work in Literacy

See Eisner's *The Arts and the Creation of Mind* for more on this subject.

Elliott Eisner, leading U.S. theorist on art education, argues that assessment of creative work as is found in drama-led language arts classrooms is necessary.

> Without some form of assessment and evaluation the teacher cannot know what the consequences of teaching have been. Not to know, or at least not to try to know, is professionally irresponsible. And to claim that such consequences cannot in principle be known is to ask people to support educational programs on faith. (p. 179)

Assessing work in the creative arts is a contentious subject. It is hard enough to define what creativity is and how it can be recognized. To *assess* creativity is even more problematic, and some people would say it is neither possible nor necessary. Yet in the creative curriculum, it is essential to be able to say what constitutes good work and equally important to have some way of describing progress and development in these areas. If we believe that the creative arts are an essential part of education for all students, then we cannot exempt them from assessment.

The assessment of creative work, however, needs to be adequate to the task. Too much assessment involves box ticking: judging performance against a set of predetermined criteria. This kind of assessment is inadequate for any kind of complex learning but particularly inappropriate for the assessment of a creative subject such as drama, which involves imagination, original thinking, and interpretation. Creative learning needs creative approaches to assessment.

Here are three examples of such approaches.

Self-assessment and reflection

In recent years self-assessment has been recognized as a key way of improving students' work. Indeed, self-assessment is essential if learning is to take place. Self-assessment encourages reflection; students learn to consider how their work is improving, what evidence their judgment is based on, and what they still need to work on. Self-assessment of this kind is continuous and is part of the learning process. Teachers also learn from hearing how students see their own progress.

But if self-assessment is too constrained by predetermined learning objectives, then students will be limited in what they focus on, and the opportunity for looking in detail at their individual learning will be lost. Students need to be involved in the framing of criteria for self-assessment; unless they are able to develop an understanding of what the criteria mean, they will not be in a position to assess their own learning. Most important, some of the criteria used in arts assessment need to be broad and qualitative, enabling students to look at their learning as a whole and describe its particular qualities. Particularly in arts subjects, it is essential that assessment not limit what students can learn by focusing too narrowly on individual skills and competencies.

Portfolio assessment and electronic portfolios

Portfolio assessment, a particularly effective way to encourage reflection and self-assessment in students, lends itself readily to assessment in the arts. Students can keep their own portfolios, in which they include both direct evidence of their work in a creative arts subject and their own commentary on this work. The work of Harvard University's Arts Propel project was pioneering in this field. This important project on the use of portfolios in arts assessment was part of Project Zero, set up in 1967 to study learning, thinking, and creativity in the arts. For several years, Project Zero was directed by Prof. Howard Gardner.

The portfolio assessment approach obviously lends itself well to work in the visual arts, but it can easily be adapted for use in the drama curriculum. Students record regular samples of their work in drama through photography or audio recording, including them with commentaries in their portfolios. Choosing the particular samples is an important aid to reflection, and commenting in detail on what a particular sample shows about their work enables students to further develop their capacity for reflection and critical analysis.

Discussions with the teacher about what to include in a portfolio and about the individual items in any given portfolio enable students to build an assessment vocabulary appropriate to a particular arts subject.

With modern digital photography, video, and recording possibilities, electronic portfolios are now a really practical possibility. Modern students find it straightforward to use these forms of recording. This kind of portfolio, where the commentary is orally recorded, can be particularly helpful for students who are comfortable with talking through their work, but find it much more challenging to provide extended written commentary.

A model for creative learning

One model that has helped some teachers to think about students' creative learning and how well they as teachers are addressing it is the six-strand Creative Learning Assessment continuum. This model of the development of creative learning evolved as part of a project on the assessment of creative learning by the Centre for Literacy in Primary Education (CLPE). The Centre is based in London, in the United Kingdom.

1. *Confidence, independence, enjoyment.* This strand recognizes that students' feelings and attitudes are fundamental to their learning progress. If students are confident learners, prepared to venture and take risks, if they enjoy and are engaged in their creative learning, they are likely to make progress.
2. *Collaboration and communication.* Much creative learning involves students in working effectively together, sometimes within a team; they need to be able to carry out joint arts projects and evolve solutions together. For this they need to be able to communicate and to present their ideas both to each other and to other audiences.
3. *Creativity.* This strand recognizes the importance of imagination and originality in learning. It also focuses attention on students' ability to generate and play with ideas, to make connections and solve problems.
4. *Strategies and skills.* Teachers can look at children's growing ranges of creative skills, some of them generic and others specific to a particular creative subject, and see how these are evident in students' creative work.
5. *Knowledge and understanding.* This strand looks at students' developing knowledge of particular art forms and creative subjects. Teachers can consider how students are mastering the technical languages of particular art forms and how their increasing knowledge is informing their own creative work.
6. *Reflection and evaluation.* Here, the continuum provides an opportunity to assess students' growing ability to reflect on their own creative work and respond to that of others. Their developing knowledge will help them to be more analytical and more helpfully critical in their reflective judgments.

A complete system of assessment of students' creative work in the arts, Creative Learning Assessment draws on tried and tested approaches to qualitative assessment based on observation and record keeping. It contains observational frameworks to help teachers note the learning development of children engaged in creative projects. It also incorporates a Creative Learning Scale, which enables teachers to arrive at agreed-upon judgments of students' progress.

The following diagram shows the intertwining within the continuum.

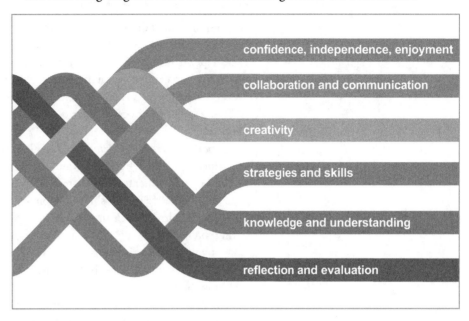

Creative Learning Assessment continuum, as developed by the Centre for Literacy in Primary Education, United Kingdom

When Students Work in Role

Working in role is a powerful way of learning. By becoming the story and by standing in other people's shoes, students can gain access to a wider range of feelings, thoughts and ideas, and knowledge. This imaginative engagement deepens their appreciation of texts, making them more imaginative and empathetic learners. It also helps their writing — they are able to move into new areas of language and to try out different registers.

By observing and recording what happens when students learn through role, teachers can gain more evidence not only of their learning, but also of what works. In this way, they can develop the use of role in their own teaching. In the rest of this book, we show how to create a wide range of opportunities for working in role. For some teachers, the ideas and techniques will be new, and they may be unsure of how to begin: this book sets out to show them how.

Centre for Literacy in Primary Education: Acknowledgments

Part A of this book draws on the research and development, and the publications of the Centre for Literacy in Primary Education (CLPE) in London, United Kingdom (www.clpe.co.uk). We therefore wish to acknowledge our debt to CLPE and to the innovative and creative research carried out by CLPE staff and teachers involved in action research projects and courses.

In particular, we are grateful for permission to draw on the work described in the following:

- *Animating Literacy: Inspiring Children's Learning Through Teacher and Artist Partnerships*, edited by Sue Ellis and Kimberly Safford (published by CLPE in 2005). This book documents the outcomes of a year-long action research project, sponsored by Creative Partnerships London South.

- *Assessing Learning in Creative Contexts* by Sue Ellis, Myra Barrs, and Jane Bunting (published in July 2007; available to download at www.clpe.co.uk/research/creativity-projects/assessing-creativity). This document is the final report of an action research project led by CLPE with Lambeth City Learning Centre and CfBT Action Zone.

- "The Assessment of Creative Learning," a paper by Sue Ellis and Myra Barrs in *Creative Learning*, edited by Julian Sefton Green (published by Creative Partnerships/Arts Council England in 2008).

- *BookPower 6: Literacy Through Literature* by Jane Bunting, Deborah Nicholson, Sue McGonigle, and Myra Barrs (published by CLPE in 2011). This guide supports teachers in using books as the centre of a literacy program and draws on examples from classrooms.

- *Boys on the Margin: Promoting Boys' Literacy Learning at Key Stage 2* by Kimberly Safford, Olivia O'Sullivan, and Myra Barrs (published by CLPE in 2004). This classroom research project featured the work of several London teachers.

- *The Reader in the Writer: The Links Between the Study of Literature and Writing Development at Key Stage 2* by Myra Barrs and Valerie Cork (published by CLPE in 2001). This report presents the findings of a two-year classroom-based research project to study the effects on children's writing of their reading of literary texts.

PART B
Demonstrations, Strategies, and Texts for Role-Playing

In the seven chapters that follow, we explore the conventions, structures, and strategies that help us to develop units of work that will promote student engagement, artistic action inside forms of drama, and personal reflection about the issues, about how drama functions, and about the way to learn from being both inside and outside the work. We need to be aware of all the concerns that theatre reflects and those that frame our students' personal and social lives — race, social–cultural backgrounds, gender and identity, experiences, age, abilities, and interests.

Students will be both participants and spectators — sometimes both at once — as they express, interpret, shape, and share their ideas and feelings, alongside their classmates, in and out of role, negotiating and constructing meaning through this art form. They will be working in theatre's symbolic definition of time, space, and human relationships, sometimes in roles close to their own, at other times in roles very different from their lived experiences.

In these chapters, we use a variety of *conventions*, which offer a *repertoire of forms* drawn from theatre, along with co-operative activities that offer ways in which to create dramatic action. By so doing, students can try out roles and ideas, and explore issues, interpretations, and responses.

We have also provided classroom models of conventions "in action," giving a context for how and when different conventions can be used and incorporated effectively, depending on the needs, wants, and experiences of the students. These conventions can help us as teachers and the students to

- establish a context for the drama work (games as pretext)
- turn a story into action (voice-over narration as students improvise)
- create and represent symbolic and artistic moments (writing a letter in role)
- manage the energy and social relations of the players (slow-motion movement)
- motivate and inspire the group (brainstorming)
- involve different players in different ways (alter ego)
- learn about the workings of theatre from inside the experience (re-enactment)
- reflect as the drama progresses and then afterwards (role on the wall)
- change direction and refocus (teacher-in-role)
- alter meanings and perceptions (a whole-group debate)
- deepen a mood or build atmosphere (creating a soundscape)
- balance participant and spectator roles (circular theatre)
- build belief and commitment (hot-seating)
- keep students inside the agreed-upon drama context (forum theatre)

Each section in a chapter is developed around a text, a source for exploring drama. We have used all of these sources in our own work, or we have observed teachers

We wish to acknowledge Jonothan Neelands and Tony Goode for their valuable work in the book, *Structuring Drama Work*, a key resource for drama conventions.

in classrooms exploring them with their students. We present them as a way of seeing the conventions in action and of noticing how drama activity can be organized so that students work effectively and creatively in constructing drama events. The most important qualities of a resource lie in its connections to the students' interests and imaginations, and how we can exploit its potential to move students into dramatic action and behaviors.

The suggestions that accompany the units can help support the students into moving into here-and-now imagined situations and events, where the work flows between real-life actions (planning, rehearsing, organizing) and symbolic action (role-playing, improvising, moving).

Here, you can see the teacher's mind at work, setting up the context for drama, incorporating a convention, observing students' actions, refocusing with another convention, structuring the work with student partners, small groups, and the whole class, causing them to reflect within the action of the drama, redirecting the energy of the participants with a quieting activity, involving written work while in role to cohese the various group actions, using teacher-in-role to add tension, taking time to see how the drama has been developing, so that the work can continue next time.

You may work with the source or with another similar text, but always be careful to recognize your own students' requirements so that the subsequent drama will belong to them. Perhaps you will adapt suggestions of structures and strategies, and ways to implement them, from the experiences described in this book. You may find that these can support your own drama lessons and events. In any event, the ideas presented here should help your students become stronger role players and meaning makers, better communicators with their classmates, and more effective interpreters and artists in the world of theatre.

5

Joining in the Learning

The goals of games and drama are sometimes closely related. Both games and drama involve rules, fun, and learning; they require intervention, co-operation, and concentration; they ask students to participate naturally in something they enjoy doing. This chapter explores moving from games into drama.

Games in the Context of Drama

Drama games that provide students with opportunities to role-play in social situations and to explore unfamiliar relationships give students a means of practising on their own, and within their own social contexts, patterns that will be important in their adult lives. They formalize human interaction processes. As in drama, the players are constantly reversing roles — chasing or being chased, leading or following, shouting or listening — all of which promotes understanding of social actions and counteractions.

Games and activities that generate movement, co-operation, and participation can be used in all aspects of drama learning.

- Sometimes, games work as physical warmups before the actual drama begins. A game that promotes teamwork can model how the main drama event will be organized.
- Sometimes, games can be used near the end of a class to change the atmosphere, or to help everyone relax before the next class. An activity in which students reflect in pairs on the meanings accrued during a very physical and energetic drama event can redirect the talk and focus the class before dismissal.
- At other times, games can be used within the drama lesson for a specific purpose, such as determining or understanding the conflict at the heart of the drama situation.
- A game can lead to a dramatic exploration, where students extend the activity into an improvised event. For example, the words of a game can become the chant the players adopt as they return to the deliberations at the centre of the drama. The students might deepen drama work by enacting a dance ritual, distancing the conflict within the improvisation through another mode of experience. They can chant while sitting in a circle, with the sound getting louder as the hunter nears the hunted. They can drum on the floor to accompany the movements or shake rattles or tambourines. They can wear masks or makeup, or you can change the lighting or use the sound created by a metal sheet to indicate thunder and lightning.

On the next page is an outline of one dramatic game, Dead One, Arise! The appendix outlines several more games and activities. We hope that playing any of the games we outline will enable students to actively engage in co-operative activities that support the drama events that follow.

Dead One, Arise!

We have used this game with all ages because it holds all the elements of the drama experience in its frame — tension, excitement, surprise, and full participation. Variations of the game are found in Sicily, Czechoslovakia, and Germany.

1. Ask the players to identify different reasons for going to a graveyard, for example, power. The ring on the dead one's hand is powerful; if they remove it, they will then have power.
2. Choose one person to lie on the ground and be covered with a blanket, sheet, or pile of jackets. The rest of the participants walk round the body, calling solemnly, "Dead One, arise! Dead One, arise! Dead One, arise!" No one can touch the body, and everyone pretends not to look at it. Then, when least expected, the "dead" person answers the call. He or she rushes at those who have been calling out and tries to touch someone.
3. When someone is caught, he or she joins the "dead" body. The game continues until everyone is part of the dead body. Options include adding music and performing the game in slow motion. The game can be repeated with drumming added while the players chant, "Dead One, arise!"

Alternative — Grandmother's Footsteps: Here is another version of the game. Suspense, the challenge of keeping the body in control, the excitement of figuring out tactics to succeed, and the fun of taking calculated risks all contribute to the game's popularity. You can watch the game in action on www.youtube.com.

1. One person volunteers to be Grandmother, or It. He or she stands, with back to the players, at one end of the playing space.
2. Have the other players form a line at the opposite end of the playing space, facing Grandmother's back.
3. The players try to creep up on Grandmother but must freeze if he/she turns. Grandmother can turn whenever she/he feels like it, and anyone caught moving must return to the starting line and begin again.
4. The player who successfully reaches and touches Grandmother wins and becomes the next Grandmother.

Touch of Power

In introducing a drama about ordinary folk contending with a powerful authority figure, the class might play this game with the word *grandmother* replaced by *sorceress* or *king*. The players try to touch this figure and thereby become the leader.

Dramatic Rituals

Rituals are often believed to have special power, and the way in which the ritual is performed takes on great symbolic significance. Ancient rituals brought individuals together so that all thoughts and energies would be focused on one activity. Everyone behaved in the same way and worked towards the same goal. The group experience took over, and an understanding that was shared by all was created. Through ritual, the knowledge and beliefs of the society were passed on to future generations.

Ritual is very important to drama. Indeed, early rituals were the beginning of formal theatre. The duties of the priest and other participants in the ritual gradually became roles taken on by actors; the other members of the group went from being worshippers to audience members. The forms of past rituals offer students involved in drama a way of adding power to their work, focusing the improvised playing with a careful structure that can add solemnity or choreographed movement to the event being explored. Games often retain elements of older rituals.

You can create your own rituals with the students and use these as part of a drama you are creating, or as the beginning or ending of your drama. In a drama about fishers lost at sea, for example, there might be this ritual: the whole village stands at the dock, and one by one, each family member tosses an object owned by a lost sailor into the ocean. Often, the drama lesson resembles ritual, where participants co-operate with each other, address a single focus, and strive for an emotional joining-in of all involved. Of course, this work is not incorporating authentic rituals because students are role-playing the events and believing as actors.

Capturing the Bear — from game to ritual

In the past, people would celebrate an event by replaying it through an art form as thanks to the higher spirits who guided them, in tribute to any who lost their lives during the event, or even as a prediction of a successful experience next time. Although the origin of the ritual has likely been lost, as in many children's games, the remaining pieces form a kind of ritual that embodies the spirit of the original experience. In the following game, you will find remnants of past events with hunters and prey, and through drama, students can create their own context for the hunt.

1. Invite everyone to sit on chairs in a large circle. The greater the diameter of the circle, the greater fun the game will be. The success of the game depends on total silence and stillness from the onlookers.
2. Select two people, one as the Hunter and the other as the Bear. Two helpers blindfold both and take them to opposite sides of the circle. They turn each player around three times. The helpers then return to their places.
3. The game begins when there is complete quiet, and (to build up the feeling of ceremony), a leader says, "Night has fallen." The Hunter and the Bear then begin to move. The Hunter should be encouraged to listen for the whereabouts of the Bear so that the Bear can be more easily caught. Both players must keep moving, and the rest of the group must steer the players gently back into the circle if they move towards the edges. To add to the ritual, the Bear could be made to wear a bell. The "bear," when captured, can choose the next player.
4. *Building the Drama:* This game can be turned into a dramatic ritual by using some of the following questions to determine the aspects of the hunt that will remain in the created ritual developed by the class. Elements of past rituals may emerge in answer to the questions, and new ritualistic moments can be created through the decisions taken by the class. As the work develops, the dramatic aspects will become more complex; eventually, a scenario is constructed and it becomes a theatrical event.

Questioning
   - Will the Bear be represented by a single person, a pair, or a small group?
   - How will the Bear move? What will it sound like?
   - How will the Hunter be portrayed?
   - What are some other roles that the participants could take?
   - Will there be standing? crouching? leaping? prowling?
   - Will there be dancing?

- Will class members imitate the Bear's actions?
- How will the space be used? Will you call for a circle or line?
- How will the Hunter(s) approach the Bear? close in on the Bear? capture the Bear?
- Will you use a drum or any other instrument to beat a rhythm?
- Will any props, costumes, or makeup be used to enhance the ritual?
- Can you create masks for the ritual?
- How can students create the fierceness and bravery of the Hunter?
- What nonverbal sounds will they use? grunts? growls? moans? humming?
- Will there be any words?
- Will there be places of silence? time to rest?
- Will the ritual include the killing of the Bear? If so, how will it be handled?
- Will there be some group work that will then be made part of the whole class's presentation of the ritual?
- How will the class end the ritual? Quietly? With a shout? Fading out? Building up? With music or chant?

Ceremonies of Celebration

A ceremony is a formal act or set of formal acts established by custom or authority as part of a special occasion, such as a wedding or religious rite. Students can develop their own ceremonies as part of a drama lesson where words, songs, dance, and movement represent an invented scenario that has the effect of appearing as a ceremony. For example, how will the villagers present their gifts to the king so that he will respect them and treat them fairly? Will they bow each time? When addressing the monarch, will they speak appropriately? Will they choose only the men, or will women be allowed to approach the king as well?

The poem that follows offers opportunities to create four, interconnected ceremonies to celebrate nature, as many past societies did, and perhaps as we still do with winter festivals and summer athletic games.

Ceremonies for four seasons

1. Divide the class into four groups. Each group will work on one verse of the text representing a season of weather and will work out a ceremony.
2. When each group has determined its ceremony, have it consider how to include the rest of the class in its work. For example, is there a place where other students can join in the chanting or in the movement?

Below, the text of the poem is accompanied by a summary of questions that each group could consider.

The Forces of Nature

[1] **Rain, *Clouds*, Rain!**

Choral Dramatization

Rain, Clouds, rain!
Fill the rain barrel
and the sandbox.
Make the river sing!
Wash away the dust of winter,

Group #1: Rain

– How will your group be seated?
– Which levels will you use?
– Which actions will you repeat?
– Will you mirror the actions; that is, will you follow a leader?

clean the sidewalks
and the tired road.
Look! The windows shine.
The rain sparkles the world.
There are diamonds
dripping from the sky.

Water the plants!
Water the trees!
Tell the flowers to poke
their heads up
from their sleep.
Feed the leaves
that are reborn in spring.
Give us grass to soften our steps,
and puddles for splashing.
Rain, Clouds, rain!

- What rhythm will you use?
- How will you begin the ceremony?
- How will you end the ceremony?

[2] Blow, *Wind*, Blow!

Blow, Wind, blow!
Strip all the leaves
from the trees.
Turn plastic bags into kites
that will fly into next year.
Warn all the children
that winter's in sight.
Give them a fright.
Rattle the windows
and shake all the doors!
Run through the town
Turn us upside down!

Control yourself, Wind.
Don't try too hard.
Keep all the hurricanes
and the tornadoes
far away from my yard!
We know how strong you can be
when you decide to run wild.
Remember your cousin—
the warm breeze
who cools us in the summer evening.
Hey! You stole my hat!
Go, Wind, go!

Group #2: Wind

- When will you speak loudly? softly?
- When will words or phrases be repeated?
- Will any words be echoed?
- Will you use the call-and-response technique, where a speaker calls out each line and the participants repeat it together?
- Will any parts be said solo? in pairs? in small groups? by the whole group?

[3] Fall, *Snow*, Fall!

Fall, Snow, fall!
Over our ankles,
up to our knees!
Cover the trees!
Blanket the earth!

Group #3: Snow

- What rhythm will you use?
- What choral techniques will you use: solos, duets, small groups, large groups?
- Will you use real instruments?

Deeper, deeper,
until we are trapped
inside the house.
Close the school!
Turn the hill
into a slide.
Cover the fields —
far and wide.

Hide the shovels!
Find the parkas
and rubber boots,
the woolen hats
the scarves that wind about us.
Let us make patterns
and tracks in the white.
May it snow all day, snow all night.
There's not enough snow
at all, at all . . .
Fall, Snow, fall!

– Will you use invented
  instruments?
– Will you use any recorded music?
– Will your use of sound and song
  be constant?
– How can you help create a mood?

[4] Shine, *Sun*, Shine!

Shine, Sun, shine!
Warm the world,
and heat up the lake.
We shall swim all day
until we turn into wrinkles.
Make the sand warm under our toes,
for who knows?
We may dig a hole
to the other side of the world.
Just try to melt my ice cream —
I can lick it faster!

We know you are strong,
O king of the sky!
But we are ready, too.
My sunscreen protects me
against you!
Do you see my sun hat?
Can you see my eyes
behind my sunglasses?
When I hide under
the umbrella,
Where are you?
When you hide behind
the cloud,
we still feel your heat.
The sand burns our feet . . .
Shine, Sun, shine!

— David Booth

Group #4: Sun

– What props will you use?
– What costumes will you use?
– Will you use masks? makeup?
– How will you create and use
  space?
– Will you use any special lighting?
– What mood do you wish to
  create, and how can you
  artistically assist in creating this
  mood?

3. After the individual groups have arrived at decisions on how to implement their tasks, discuss ways to assemble all the elements. The ceremony can be presented with the whole class working together. Eventually, let students incorporate theatre crafts such as instruments, props, costumes, masks, makeup, and lighting.

Teaching Technique: **Maintaining Control**

It takes time to learn how to manage an interactive and improvisational drama experience. These suggestions may help.

- A circle is an excellent control technique. The teacher has a total view of the class and can speak to each student across the circle. There is a unity to the group, everyone is equal in the space, and the centre of the circle can become an immediate area for demonstration.
- A signal for freezing will also aid in controlling a class. For example, a tambourine can be struck or rattled to indicate that the group should stand still, frozen to the spot. This signal must not be overused, but it can help improve the students' concentration.
- Asking the students to work in slow motion, as in a dream, may help control movement, improve concentration, and increase involvement.
- Intervening, arresting, or stopping the action of the drama allows the teacher to listen to the students' ideas, clarify the situation, deepen the context, define or redefine the focus, build belief, achieve a consensus within the group, deal with conflicting emotions, or allow time for reflection.
- Replaying a scene allows new ideas to be added and encourages refining and polishing for a final synthesis of the ideas that have been explored. If sharing is a goal, the drama should be replayed with energy and new learning rather than as a rehearsed scene.

Movement Messages

Activities involving movement can help students learn how to express their feelings and ideas through their bodies and through interacting physically with the members of the group. Learning to communicate through movement can bring physical confidence and the ability to tell a story in situations where words alone are not effective. Many of the movement activities in drama are co-operative efforts and involve learning to trust others. Sometimes, students move by themselves, sometimes with others. They can also experiment with gestures, facial expressions, and body language.

By moving to music, by responding to the rhythm, tempo, and structure of music and sound, students can deepen and extend the aesthetic power of the drama activity. Dance drama does not require the technical aspects of dance. Rather, the patterns of dance-like movement are blended with the story being told in the drama. Sometimes, dance drama is used within the drama to convey the conflict of the story, to show an event from the past, or to picture a dream. The music chosen as stimulus can be selected from movie soundtracks, classical pieces that create an atmosphere, drumming or sound instruments performed by the students, or songs such as folk songs or rhythm and blues recorded or sung by participants. Often, students will provide suggestions for music or sound to accompany or complement the drama work.

Some powerful work can be done incorporating movement and dance drama using games, myth, legend, ceremonies, and rituals. Because these kinds of structures tell so much with so few details, students might elaborate upon the few facts given to incorporate movement as the mode for expressing or interpreting. Use of makeup, masks, costumes, and chanting can add to the power of the work. For example, a bolt of blue cloth can suggest a river, the sky, or a path to eternity.

The featured activities engage students in building patterns for group creations.

Moving in patterns

1. Students form a large circle. Every second person steps forward to make an inner circle. The circles move in opposite directions with rhythmic movement of feet — one-two-three-stop, one-two-three-stop, and so on. Students count aloud.
2. Students could chant selected words that the group has agreed upon (perhaps the rhyme "Hickory Dickory Dock"). Or, participants could count in another language, such as French.
3. Students add a movement, such as lifting an arm up on one set of beats and lowering it on the next set. Both circles can perform the movement together, or one circle can raise arms as the other circle lowers arms. Students can gradually speed up the rhythm, perhaps to the beat of a drum. They finish on "freeze."

Creating a monster

Creating a monster is much the same as developing a machine. One by one, in no special order, students come forward, adding movements and sounds that in some way fit in with the actions already started by other players. The class's object in this exercise is to create a sinister creature that would cause some sort of unpleasantness for anyone who gets in its way. The students do not plan beforehand how the monster will look or sound when fully created.

Remind students that a monster is a living thing, not a machine. Like any real living creature, a monster should have some symmetry between its right and left sides. Suppose, for example, that a player begins the game by kneeling and moving her right arm forward and back at shoulder level, suggesting some sort of antenna. A second player might then kneel beside the first, facing the same direction, and perform the same action with his left arm. Each action and sound added should help suggest the monster's menacingly sinister qualities. A gesture might be claw-like; a foot movement might be a powerful thud. The monster should be able to move — walking, creeping, or slithering — about the room.

Consider doing the activity in groups of 4, then 8, then 16, and eventually with the whole class creating one monster.

Games, rituals, ceremonies, and movement can both contribute to the power of drama under construction and enable our students to better work out understandings of drama. We can add to our repertoire of strategies for building and strengthening drama by incorporating them into our programs as elements that contribute to the collaborative and aesthetic power of the drama we are constructing. We can also use them as forms for exploring and interpreting drama, offering our students ways and means of shaping ideas and feelings, responses, and inventive suggestions into a theatre form.

6

The Storyteller Arrives

Retelling a story can enrich and extend students' personal hoard of words, ideas, stories, songs, and concepts, and deepen their understanding and appreciation of literature. Retelling increases students' mastery of language by showing them that words can be manipulated into new meanings. It helps students actively internalize language structures and styles. It develops the ability to turn narration into dialogue and dialogue into narration. It encourages role-playing, which, in turn, provides students with valuable practice in shifting points of view and in experimenting with different styles of language and a variety of voices. Retelling can provide the initial starting point for the drama. It can reveal an unexplained idea in even a well-known story. It can focus details. It can be review of what has already taken place, or it can serve as a way of building reflection in role.

Engaging Students in Retelling

There are many ways to help students learn to retell stories.

- Students can retell stories in a circle, or with a partner. You can provide opportunities for them to change the story, or find the new stories within the story.
- Using wordless picture books, students can describe in their own words what they see happening, sometimes supplying the characters with what they feel is appropriate dialogue.
- As a student retells a tale, signal for someone to continue the story or allow another child to take over at a dramatic pause in the story.
- When you recount a story, pause every so often, and point to someone in the group to add an appropriate word. "Once upon a time there was a young . . ." "He walked until suddenly . . ." "He said . . ."
- Holding a "talking stick" can give a student the right to speak. The "talking stick" is passed on to the next student when the speaker stops (which can even be in mid-phrase).
- One student retells to a partner a story in role which the teacher told; then, the second student tells the story back in another role to the first student.
- One student begins telling a story. The object is to get to the end of the story without being distracted by the partner. As a variant, the students work in groups of three. Two students tell stories simultaneously and compete for the attention of the third.
- Each student in a small group reads the same story silently. When students have finished, number them off. On a pre-arranged signal, student 1 from each group begins to retell until the signal sounds. Student 2 takes over, then student 3, and so on — in this way the story is retold with no one student responsible. Students can retell from various points of view or try multipart

narration, where one narrator shapes the tale while others retell from their chosen points of view. Finally, students can get inside the story by exploring a challenging or magical part, creating a chant or rhyme to "help" the characters out of difficulty.

A story to tell: "The Shoemaker and the Elves"

It is best to truly tell a traditional story like this rather than read it off a page.

There was a shoemaker once who made very fine shoes, but up until now he had been plain unlucky. It didn't seem to matter how hard he worked. He just got poorer and poorer. Soon he couldn't buy enough leather and materials to make shoes.

One Sunday night, he laid out his tools and his last piece of leather on the workbench.

"Perhaps if I get up early I can make one pair of shoes and try to sell them." Then heaving a big sigh, he went sadly to bed.

When he entered his shop Monday morning, the leather was nowhere to be seen, but on the workbench was a pair of shoes in the latest fashion. The astonished shoemaker took them outside into the light and held them up. They were completely finished down to the last seam and there wasn't a poor stitch in them. The shoemaker ran back into the shop to fetch his wife.

"What's happened?" she said.

"Come quickly." They ran into the shop. The shoemaker held up the shoes. "Will you look at this! Someone has done us a great kindness."

"Well, don't stand there gawking, man. Put them in the window. Let's see if we can sell them," said his wife.

It just happened that a passer-by looked in the window as the shoemaker was placing the shoes. She entered the shop, inspected the shoes, and was so pleased with the quality and style of the work she bought them.

"Work this fine deserves more than you're asking," she said. And the woman paid the shoemaker handsomely.

Now the shoemaker had enough money to buy leather for two pairs of shoes. On Monday night he laid out his tools and the leather and went peacefully to bed.

When he entered the shop on Tuesday morning, there were two pairs of shoes on the workbench, beautifully made and ready for sale. The shoemaker's hammer, awl, knife, wax, thread, needles, and pegs were scattered about the workbench as though someone was working there, but there was no one to be seen.

"I don't know what is happening," exclaimed the shoemaker, "but it's a miracle!" That morning he sold both pairs of shoes and the satisfied customers gladly gave him more money than he was asking. Now he had enough money to buy leather for four pairs of shoes. And so it continued, night after night. The delighted shoemaker would set out his leather, and each morning newly made shoes appeared in the shop.

Day after day customers came and paid such high prices that the shoemaker was able to buy a good quantity of leather. More and more shoes got made. More and more shoes got sold. More and more money filled the shoemaker's pockets.

One night as the shoemaker set out enough leather for twenty-four pairs of shoes, his wife said, "I am so curious to know what happens in here while we're asleep. Why don't we hide in the shop tonight and try to find out who it is who is doing us this kindness?"

And so they did. The shoemaker and his wife pushed a clothes rack full of clothes into the shop and hid behind it.

Bong! Bong! Bong! The clock began to strike the midnight hour. Everything was still. Suddenly two tiny elves bounced into the room. They were naked. They didn't have a stitch of clothing on. They leaped onto the workbench and without so much as a word set to work. Their fingers fairly flew as they bored holes, pulled thread and hammered away with a rap tap, tap tap, tack, tack, tack.

The shoemaker and his wife couldn't believe their eyes. The elves worked swiftly and skillfully and soon twenty-four pairs of shoes were finished down to the last stitch. Then in the blink of an eye, the elves sprang up and dashed away.

The shoemaker's wife was speechless. When she finally found her words, she said, "I feel terrible. Those poor wee things have made us rich, but did you notice, they can't even afford clothes. We must help them. We must show our thanks and kindness."

"What do you have in mind?" asked the shoemaker. "I don't think they'll take our money."

"I have it," said his wife, "I've got scraps of cloth, enough ends of yarn to make them little sweaters and trousers, maybe even hats. You must make them some shoes."

And that's what they did.

When everything was ready, the shoemaker and his wife laid out sweaters, hats, trousers, and shoes. Then they hid behind the clothes rack.

At midnight the elves skipped in to begin work. They looked around. They saw no leather. Instead, they saw two sweaters, two pair of trousers, two woolen hats with tassels, and four leather shoes with pointy toes.

The elves looked at each other. Their faces wore puzzled looks. Then it dawned on them. The clothes were for them. They snatched up the clothes and dressed themselves. Then they started dancing around laughing and singing at the top of their voices.

"Now we are handsome gentlemen. Why should we ever work again?"

Then dressed from tasseled hats to pointy shoes, they began to skip and run about like wild things. They leaped over chairs, dove in and out of drawers, then stood on the spot and started spinning like tops. Suddenly they stopped twirling, gave a great screech, and flew out the door.

They never came back, but the shoemaker and his wife had no regrets, and they were always lucky after that.

Picturing the story

A teacher told the story "The Shoemaker and the Elves" to her Grade 3 class. She planned to do some story retelling with them, but before doing that, she invited the students to revisit the story in their imaginations and to share with the class anything they had noticed as they listened.

At first, some students were silent. They didn't quite know how to answer, but after a few gentle prompts, observations were made. Most agreed that they had made pictures in their minds and offered examples. ("I saw the bit where the elves were running around like crazy at the end.")

The teacher pressed the students to recall mental pictures in greater detail. "Did anyone make a picture of the shoes made by the elves? Did anyone notice the colors of the sweaters made by the shoemaker's wife?" More and more personal experiences of the story emerged. Questions were posed. "If the elves were magic, why wouldn't they know the shoemaker and his wife were spying on them?" "Did elves really exist?" Memories were shared. "I saw this story done by the Muppets only they changed a lot of stuff." This comment led the students into discussion of picture book versions they had experienced and other stories about shoes, boots, and the supernatural.

When the students had finished telling the stories of their listening, the teacher had them find partners. She handed out large sheets of newsprint to each pair and asked them to draw the story. These students had done a lot of story mapping in class, and many set to work retelling the story that way. A few students divided the paper into equal segments and created a storyboard. One pair drew a large pair of very fancy shoes in the middle of the paper then sketched key story moments around the shoes as they pieced the tale together.

The work described here is important to the eventual success of the story retelling — this is a very effective rehearsal strategy.

When the drawing phase had concluded, the teacher asked the students to face each other with the drawing between them. The students were labeled A and B and informed that A would begin to tell the story to B in his or her own words, pretending that B had never heard it before. The teacher explained that after 30 seconds, she would ring a bell to signal that it was student B's turn to take over and continue the telling, and so on. She also stressed that in the activity, good listening was as important as telling and that the teller should not be interrupted or ignored.

Some students finished way ahead of others and the teacher had them begin again, making sure to take time to make everything happen.

Making images — Whoosh!

At the conclusion of the story retelling, the teacher observed that much of the picturing the students had described from their listening wasn't happening in the retelling. She chose to introduce a game called Whoosh!, which encourages participants to concentrate on making images. She sat the students in a circle and explained that she would tell the story "The Shoemaker and the Elves" again and that they could all participate in the telling. As the story proceeded, any who wished could enter the circle, taking on the shape and acting out what was being described.

"All you must do is listen to the story, and be and do what the story says," she said. "When I say 'Whoosh!' anyone in the centre of the circle must leave immediately and sit back in your place. You can participate as much as you like."

The teacher began by reminding the students of the cast of characters. "Once upon a time, there was a shoemaker and his wife, some very clever elves, and many, many satisfied shoe purchasers." Students entered the playing space and mimed being elves, customers, or shoemakers. When the teacher said, "Whoosh!" they quickly left the space to await the next bit of the story.

Discovering stories within the story

In the days to follow, the teacher engaged the students in drama activities that brought to light stories to be found inside "The Shoemaker and the Elves."

- The students made still images (see the Glossary, "Overview of Drama Conventions") in groups that represented the bad luck the shoemaker and his wife had experienced.
- The students conducted interviews in pairs with the customer who bought the first pair of shoes. They worked on the notion that these couldn't have been ordinary shoes. What was it about them that had so intrigued the buyer and moved her to pay more?
- The students hot-seated, or interviewed, the teacher-in-role as the shoemaker's wife to find out what materials she had on hand when she decided to clothe the elves and to describe the final outfits. Some questions of interest to the students were as follows:
  1. Because of the elves your bad luck changed. What did you learn from the elves that made things better?
  2. Were the elves thankful for the clothes, or were they making fun of you?
  3. If you could do it again, would you still make the clothes, or would you try something different?
  4. Did you try anything to get the elves to come back?

  The teacher-in-role couldn't answer the second question, so formed the students into a corridor of voices (see the Glossary, "Overview of Drama Conventions") and then walked through as the students suggested other possibilities. (Examples: "The elves were cross because you made the clothes out of old scraps." "You need sparkly stuff to dress elves.")
- Customers were willing to pay more than the price indicated on the price tag to own the shoes. But these were fairy shoes. Students discussed what might be scary, annoying, or fun about wearing these shoes. In small groups they did one-minute improvisations in which they portrayed the challenges posed by wearing such shoes.
- Students worked in groups of four. One student took the part of the third-person narrator and the others each took a first-person role (e.g., the shoemaker, an elf, a customer). A multipart retelling was attempted. The third-person narrator started off and then quickly called upon the others, one at a time, to tell the story from their viewpoint. The telling went back and forth between the narrator and the first-person tellings until the story was finished.

Side-Coach Note: Third-Person Narration

With younger students, you can model the activity by taking the part of the third-person narrator. Seat the students in a circle and assign parts: the shoemaker, the shoemaker's wife, a customer, another customer, elf one, elf two, and so on. Depending on class size, you may have triple casting or more.

Begin the story, then point to a student who then advances the story through the eyes of his or her character. When you take the story back, link the previous teller's work to that of the next teller with brief narration and point to another student.

Teaching Technique: **Narrating from Inside the Drama**

The teacher can also use narration within the drama experience
- to set the mood (Example: "The cave is growing dark. Now there is no light of any kind. Shadows loom over the lonely tribe, huddled together.")
- to cover jumps in time (Example: "What will happen 10 years from now when the tribe meets a stranger who has never heard of its problems?")
- to prepare the students for what will come next (Example: "Each member of the tribe went to his or her small private place in the cave and began to think about the past 10 years, the losses, the pain, the incidents that couldn't be forgotten.")
- to incorporate details necessary for the drama (Example: "Each member of the tribe votes by selecting a black or white pebble and placing the pebble, after careful consideration, in the hidden space by the door.")

- to make the students aware of how they have changed (Example: "The members of the tribe lie around the fire, understanding that now they solve problems not through war but through negotiation and arbitration.")
- to give import to the words and actions of the students (Example: "The tribe agrees to be governed by the dictates of the council, to accept the legislated decisions, and to comply with the requests of the chosen body.")
- to present stories from the teacher's own life (Example: "I remember when . . .")

The Storyteller's Voice

The voice of the storyteller invites us to leave the present and journey to places where wonders can occur or where we might meet strange and unusual people, such as Francesco de la Vega. A teacher read aloud the poem "Francesco de la Vega" by Charles Causley to his Grade 6 class. Afterwards, he asked the students to describe to a talk partner any pictures they made in their minds as they listened. Here is the poem.

Francesco de la Vega

[1] Francesco de la Vega
From the hours of childhood
Passed his days
In the salt of the ocean.

Only one word he spoke.
Lierjanes! — the name
Of the sea-village of his birth
In the Year of God 1657.

While other students
Helped in field or kitchen,
Wandered the mountain-slope,
He swam the wild bay.

While others were at church
He dived to where lobster and squid
Lodged in the sea's dark cellar.
He must suffer a salt death, said Father Ramiro.

His mother and father entreated him
To come to his own bed.
His brothers and sisters called him
Home from the yellow sand-bar.

Amazed, they watched him
Arrow the waves like a young dolphin.
Until they tired of waiting, he hid
Under the mountain of black water.

[2] On a night mad with storm
The waves rose high as the church tower
And beat the shore like a drum.

He did not return with the morning.

Foolish boy now he is drowned, they said.
His family added their salt tears to the ocean
As they cast on flowers and prayers.
In my opinion, he asked for it, said Father Ramiro.

Years flowed by: ten, twenty.
The village of Lierjanes forgot him.
[3] Then, miles off Cadiz, herring fishermen
Sighted, at dawning, a sea-creature.

Three days they pursued him
Through the autumn waters;
Trapped him at last in strong nets
And brought him to land.

They gazed at his silver body in wonder;
At his pale eyes, staring always ahead;
At his hair, tight, and as a red moss.
What seemed like bright scales adorned his spine.

Most marvelous of all, instead
Of nails upon his feet and hands
There grew strange shells
That glowed gently like jewels of the sea.

When they questioned him
All he would reply was, *Lierjanes!*
Wrapping him in a soft white sailcloth
They laid him on a bed of linen.

[4] A monk of Cadiz heard their story.
It is Francesco de la Vega,
The fish-boy of Lierjanes, he declared.
I shall bring him to his home and family.

Ah, but how his parents, brothers, sisters
Wept with happiness and welcomed him
With loving kisses and embraces, as though
Like Lazarus he had risen, and from a sea-grave!

But the young man returned no sign
Of love or recognition.
He gazed at them as though sightless;
Was indifferent to their sighs, their fondlings.

Long years he dwelt among them,
Never speaking, eating little,
Shifting unhappily in the decent clothes
With which they arrayed him.

[5] One morning, nine years on,
He vanished from the house and hearth-side;
Was seen no more in the village of Lierjanes.
Great was the sadness of those who loved him!

Months, years ahead, two fishermen
Hauling across the stubborn waters
Of the Bay of Asturias
Sighted a sudden sea-creature at play.

Swiftly, and with spear and net,
They followed, but he escaped them.
As he rushed through the waves they heard a cry.
Lierjanes! Lierjanes!

Recalling story events

Volunteers were asked to describe moments they pictured vividly. Next, the teacher asked the students to recall other things that came to mind as they listened: "Did this story remind you of any other stories? What questions came into your mind? Did anything puzzle you?"

The teacher read the poem again and asked the students to consider the number of episodes in the story. The class chose the following: (1) Introduction; (2) Disappearance in the Storm; (3) The Capture; (4) Back Home; (5) The Finale.

The teacher divided the class into groups of five and read the poem a third time. As the students listened, they jotted down a bare bones outline of what occurred in each of the episodes.

Within the groups, students took responsibility for one segment each. The teacher asked the students to scatter within the classroom and take five minutes to visualize everything that happened in their segments.

Telling the story from one perspective

Side-Coach Note: 30 Seconds

It helps move things along if every 30 seconds, you use a signal to indicate that the story is to be passed to the next team member. Thirty-second shifts are sufficient for each turn.

Students reconvened in their groups, and each student told his or her segment to the others in turn. Now that each group knew what its interpretation of the story sounded like, the teacher challenged the class to think of a village resident who could tell the story from a certain perspective. For example: How would the village priest tell the story?

Each group was asked to settle on one village resident. Through the eyes of that villager, the students took turns telling the story from beginning to end.

At the end of the tellings, the teacher-in-role as a detective questioned the students in their various roles in order to complete a missing person's report.

Side-Coach Note: Stepping In

Sometimes, students choose a point of view that doesn't work. Perhaps the character chosen doesn't have enough information about the story or strong enough opinions. When you see a group floundering, move in quickly and help them try another character's point of view.

After the role play, the teacher brought the students together in a circle. They were asked to take the role of poet Charles Causley and in one sentence tell why he wrote the poem. One boy, for example, said: "I lived by the sea, and the stories of seals who were thought to be human haunted me, so I wanted to write this poem." A short debriefing session followed: teacher and students shared their thoughts about some of the themes and ideas that the activity highlighted.

Moving Beyond the Story

In "The Storyteller's Voice," above, students first focused on retelling the story; then, their work evolved into retelling from one character's perspective. Here, the emphasis is on using the featured text as a springboard into a variety of literacy experiences, drama among them. The students can begin by reading "Wouldn't You Like to Know" and then discuss the feelings of poet Michael Rosen about the story of his dog. Do they have similar life stories about pets to share? You can use the concepts in the poem as sources for drama in partners, in small groups, and as a class.

Wouldn't You Like to Know

Today was not
very warm
not very cold
not very dry
not very wet.

No one round here
went to the moon
or launched a ship
or danced in the street.

No one won a great race
or a big fight.

The crowds weren't out
the bands didn't play.

There were no flags no songs
no cakes no drums.
I didn't see any processions.
No one gave a speech.

Everyone thought today was ordinary,
busy busy
in out in
hum drummer day
dinner hurry
grind away day.

Nobody knows that today
was the most special day
that has ever ever been.

Ranzo, Reuben Ranzo,
who a week and a year ago was gone
lost
straying starving
under a bus? in the canal?
(the fireman didn't know)
was here, back,
sitting on the step
with his old tongue lolling,
his old eyes blinking.

I tell you —
I was so happy
So happy I tell you
I could have grown a tail —
and wagged it.

From improvising to poetry writing

1. You might begin by brainstorming with your students all of the concerns that people have about dogs as pets in our contemporary society, and ask the students in small groups to create scenarios for dramatizing. For example, should dogs live in high-rise buildings? Should dogs wear designer clothes? Should dogs be allowed to run freely? Should all dogs wear muzzles on the street? Should we ban some breeds? How long should we wait to euthanize stray dogs? Should dogs be permitted to have pups as often and as long as owners approve?

Improvisation

2. Then, prompt students in groups to select one of these issues, which can form the basis of the improvisations they will engage in next. All the students should be inside the work at the same time, not watching others perform.

3. As teacher, you exercise a fair degree of control. You can freeze the action every so often, and ask one group to continue their conversation in role. You can change the situation whenever the students seem to have completed their scenes. You can change group members, or let the students find different partners.

4. Collect from the Internet pictures of dogs (or have students handle the search). Give each group a picture they will then use to tell the dog's story, as in the poem they have read. What roles will they select to tell the dog's life story? They could also compose a group poem using dialogue as a narrative for their dog. The poems could be shared aloud.

Playmaking: Sample scenarios for developing whole-class improvised work

It is important not to have a show-and-tell experience, but to use the contributions of groups and partners in building a thematic look at the relationships of dogs and humans. Groups can work at the same time, observing what other groups are doing only at your discretion. The object of the drama activity is to encourage complexity of thought and action on the part of the students:

- Students plead with parents to buy a dog. On what will the parents base their decision? What arguments will the students use? What tensions can be added to deepen the improvised work — allergies, the family moving, a new baby expected?
- Officials investigate complaints about a pet store and rumors that it is running a puppy mill. Those role-playing the store owners can preplan their situations; the officials can organize the complaints and questions they will have. Consider what tensions can support the role play: perhaps the officials disagree with each other or the owners bring in customers to support them.
- Neighbors have been kept awake all night by the barking of two dogs next door. What have the pet owners done to remedy the situation and why is it not working? How will the police who have been called handle the situation?
- The veterinarian has discovered the pet's illness, and the operation will cost a great deal of money the family can't afford. What if members of the family disagree on whether to proceed with the treatment? What if the dog were a stray that the family had rescued?
- Two candidates apply for the position of dog walker in a large apartment building with many dogs that need assistance. What questions will be asked by management? What qualifications will the applicants reveal?

- A city council is going to vote on the banning of certain breeds of dogs, such as mastiffs, pit bulls, and German shepherds, within the community. Some students could research the qualities of different breeds, and others could locate stories and reports of communities involved in such actions. The class can be divided into council members, who will determine the vote results; advocates for different breeds; and citizens recounting reasons and research for banning the dogs. The teacher or a guest could role-play the mayor, who will be in charge of conducting the session.

Contributions of Group Work to Whole-Class Drama Experiences

There are so many ways to let group work play a part in the growth of whole-class drama experiences.

- Each group may report back to the whole class in role (or choose a spokesperson, such as an elder).
- Each group may show a moment of the learning that members arrived at, through a tableau or an enactment of a special incident; several groups may volunteer to demonstrate some aspect of their learning.
- The groups may re-create an incident which occurred in the drama experience.
- The individuals, in a circle, may express in role their feelings about the group's work.
- As structured by the teacher, the work that goes on in groups can serve as the basis for the next part of the drama lesson; the group work may become a play within the larger context of the whole-class drama experience: a play within a play.
- Perhaps the most important time for sharing the work is when it might serve as the beginning of a drama that the whole class can then explore.

Small groups for exploring ideas

Even in the midst of a whole-class improvisation, students will need to work in pairs or in small groups from time to time in order to complete specific tasks. For example:

- There may be a need to explore several sides to a particular issue.
- The class may want to stop the drama and explore various interpretations of the problem.

Each pair or small group can present its idea, and the class can choose one as the most suitable with which to continue. Alternatively, the whole group might decide to include the thoughts of several small groups and redirect the drama.

7

Who Will I Be?

This chapter presents situations in which students learn how to observe their own lives and the lives of characters in stories and poetry. It involves students in exploring the relationship between the self and the role in creating drama. Through improvising within a drama scene, they will come to understand how dramatists work and how to find in themselves and their life experiences those moments that will help them develop, even inhabit, a role that fits into the context of the drama — the "me in the role" and "the role in me." As they explore characters within a text, students will recognize that they can empathize with them and connect with roles very different from those familiar to them. Coming to understand the motivations and behaviors of others allows students to find the secrets in themselves.

Role-Playing Through Dramatic Writing

A memoir is usually a written memory, a description of an event from the past, written in the first person, and told from one person's point of view, about one point in the author's life. It is more about the author's experience than the larger event.

The memoir reveals the feelings of the writer and shows what the person learned from the experience focused on one event. It is inherently dramatic, full of the emotional significance of this particular life incident. When developed in role, a memoir offers a vehicle for students to enter the emotional life of the role they are or were playing, a reflective opportunity for them to inhabit the situation that was the focus of the drama experience. A memoir can be read aloud after the drama as reflection, or used as information for the next part of the lesson. In the instance outlined below, students wrote in response to hearing and discussing a story.

In a combined Grade 1 and 2 classroom, the teacher read aloud the picture book *Sleeping Boy*, a modern allegory by Sonia Craddock, who uses the framework of "Sleeping Beauty" to tell the story of war, setting her narrative in Berlin. At the birthday party for Knabe Rosen, the dreaded Major Krieg arrives and predicts: "On your sixteenth birthday you will hear the drums drumming as the army marches by. Off to war you'll go — and you will not come home." But the boy's aunt, Tante Taube, gives the boy her blessing: "Instead of going off to war, Knabe Rosen will only sleep . . . sleep through poverty and war, bad times and sadness, until peace comes to Berlin."

First-person storytelling

Monologues

The students shared their responses to the story and the pictures, brought out their questions about the war and the villages, both bombed and safe, and then wrote in role as storytellers, offering their recounts and embedding their feelings in their fictional memoirs.

My villig sleept though the war. It was a mirigel rilly. If your villig got bomd i'm rilly very soory.
(My village slept through the war. It was a miracle really. If your village got bombed, I'm really sorry.)

— *Jessa*

My story is that one day I was lisanin to the radeo when I hrad a spashl brodcast war mite be starting! We proparerda for the war. I was waching out the windo I saw the bouts and planes comeing! Owe arme ran to defand our tane.
(My story is that one day I was listening to the radio when I heard a special broadcast war might be starting. We prepared for the war. I was watching out the window. I saw the boats and planes coming! Our army ran to defend our town.)

— *Andrew*

There was a Granny who blessed a wish that the child would sleep through war and her wish got mixed up and the holl village fell asleep for 5 years and all the other villages got blown up even my best friend brad maurice got blown up.
(There was a granny who blessed a wish that the child would sleep through war and her wish got mixed up and the whole village fell asleep for 5 years and all the other villages got blown up. Even my best friend Brad Maurice got blown up.)

— *Geordie*

My town got bomed and lots of people got shot. But i herd about a nother town where every body slept and when they woke up they wer un harmed it's wherede I just don't get it. How could they sleep for five years and no change age it's really wherde. One of my familly members had to go to the hospital to get surgerey.
(My town got bombed and lots of people got shot. But I heard about another town where everybody slept and when they woke up they were unharmed. It's weird. I just don't get it. How could they sleep for five years and not change age? It's really weird. One of my family members had to go to the hospital to get surgery.)

— *Adrienne*

How come your toen didet get bomed and our town did. Are forest got bomed and our hoses and apartment's are people got shot and yor's didet. I'm glad for yow.
(How come your town didn't get bombed and our town did? Our forest got bombed and our houses and apartments, our people got shot and yours didn't. I'm glad for you.)

— *Brendan*

One day a grate war hapenid. and evry persen in every town went.
(One day a great war happened, and every person in every town went.)

— *Will*

My villig as bommd. The other villig was not bommd and the other villig slept theroo a war. are villig is vary damiged.
(My village was bombed. The other village was not bombed and the other village slept through a war. Our village is very damaged.)

— *Meredith*

In their brief but heartfelt memoirs, you can observe how the first-person voice allows them to describe, recount, and comment on their perceptions of the story. The details of the story are clear in their brief retellings, and some personalize their memoirs with deep sadness or identify with the villagers who were victims of war. Their writings were first drafts since the teacher wanted their immediate responses to the heart of the allegory, but their spellings did not hold them back from using significant words and terms to portray their thoughts. Dramatic voice frees students from the constraints of many writing tasks and supports the freedom to draw upon authentic thoughts and feelings.

Opportunities to explore dramatic voice

Locating stories or picture books that employ memoirs can present great opportunities for dramatic role-playing and retelling. You can share the text, determine the roles with the students, and together choose a context for the sharing (e.g., at a ritual commemorating the ending of the war, at a dinner celebrating a character's birthday, or at a peace conference).

Memoir Picture Books

- Cooney, Barbara. *Miss Rumphius*
- Crews, Donald. *Bigmama's*
- dePaola, Tomie. *Nana Upstairs & Nana Downstairs*
- Everett, Gwen. *Li'l Sis and Uncle Willie: A Story Based on the Life and Paintings of William H. Johnson*
- Lied, Kate. *Potato: A Tale from the Great Depression*
- MacLachlan, Patricia. *All the Places to Love*
- Mitchell, Rita Phillips. *Hue Boy*
- Polacco, Patricia. *Thank You, Mr. Falker*
- Pomerantz, Charlotte. *The Chalk Doll*
- Ringgold, Faith. *Tar Beach*
- Ryder, Joanne. *My Father's Hands*
- Rylant, Cynthia. *When I Was Young in the Mountains*
- Say, Allen. *Grandfather's Journey*
- Shannon, David. *No, David!*
- Stevenson, James. *Don't You Know There's a War On?*
- Viorst, Judith. *Alexander and the Terrible, Horrible, No Good, Very Bad Day*
- Yolen, Jane. *Owl Moon*

Turning Life Experiences into Drama

We were fortunate to be part of a two-year project at an inner-city school in Toronto, where story became the focus of the students. Students from Grades 2 to 8 illustrated their particular stories under the guidance of Mark Thurman, an artist, illustrator, and writer.

Many of the students at this school come from countries where conditions of war caused their families to move to Canada. Some students, part of the first generation born in Canada, collected life stories about their parents' journeys to Canada. Some students from Canadian-born families shared stories about growing up in an urban community. Some parents told stories to their children, who then became the storytellers. The stories brought out different feelings of happiness or sadness, but all of them had a common message of pride and respect for the family.

The following examples are actual stories that the students heard from their relatives: the stuff of heritage drama created by school students. If you choose to explore heritage drama with your own class, it is a good idea to first work with any of these models. Having copies of the stories for the students will be helpful. (See Appendix B for reproducible copies in standardized English.)

The Hungry Alligator

Many, many years ago, when my grandfather was still alive, he used to work in the canals near the sugar cane fields in Guyana. He and his partner used to work very hard cleaning the weeds and grass out of the canals. No people lived back in and around the hills and there was no access to transportation or anything else. So every morning, trucks would come around to take everyone to work and then, take them all back home in the evening.

One day, my grandfather went to work with the other men as usual. He worked all day and when it was almost time to go home he was given a small area in the canal to clean out, and was attacked by an alligator. The rest of the men pulled him out, while the angry alligator pranced around. My poor grandfather nearly died that day. He was bleeding a lot from all his wounds. When the truck arrived, he was taken to hospital. Grandfather couldn't walk for weeks and he was scared for a long time from his experience but he was thankful to be still alive.

— *Sandy, Grade 4*

Coming to Canada

My mom and I came to Canada because back in Vietnam we were poor and because my aunt, uncle, grandmother and grandfather lived in Canada. My mom swore that if she could make it ever to Canada she would cut her hair off and be bald.

It all started when my mom, aunt and uncle and I left Vietnam on a boat. There were a lot of people, about 40, so we had to eat less. When we got onto the Ocean there were storms and lightning. At the time I was only 2 years old. My aunt and uncle thought they were going to die. My uncle got a rope so he, my mom, my aunt and I could tie our hands together so that if we died and floated to land people would bury us together.

But the next morning, the storm and lightning stopped. We were so happy that we hadn't died. We went to Singapore and we were separated from my aunt and uncle. We lived there for a while. Then the people from Canada came to test people to see if they knew how to speak English, but my mom failed. They sent us to the Philippines. My mom and I stayed there for 4 years. By then, my mom had my two-year-old brother and a sister, just born.

Soon after, the people from Canada came again. This time my mom passed the English test and they sent us to Canada. The church people took care of us. They gave us food and clothing. They asked if we wanted to live in a church in Mississauga. My mom said no because by then my aunt, uncle, grandmother and grandfather lived in Toronto. She wanted to be near them. The people helped us to get a house to live in because we didn't have a father and this is where we live now.

— *Van Quan, Grade 7*

My Grandfather

My granddad was born on May 11th, 1891 in Canton, China. He came to this country by boat and landed in Victoria, B.C. on January 22th 1911. He came here with his brother in search of a new life.

Life was tough for the two brothers. And life became tougher when they had to pay the Head Tax to legally stay in Canada. In 1923 that amounted to a lot of money. Granddad met his first wife who was a nanny for a rich family also from China. His first wife passed away at a very young age in Montreal.

Granddad and his brother moved from city to city in the laundry business. They had a business in Vancouver, Montreal, Toronto and Ottawa. Many Chinese people started in the laundry business because it didn't take much money to start. This was before machines, so all it took was hard work, soap and water.

Granddad was lonely for a long time because Chinese men were not allowed to sponsor families to come to Canada because of the Chinese Expulsion Act. This Act was not changed until the early 1950s. In 1954, Granddad went to Hong Kong to visit and meet my grandmom there. They got married in 1955. They came back to Canada and shortly after they settled in Ottawa and Toronto and eventually moved to northern Ontario. They lived in Kirkland Lake and Kapuskasing and eventually Hornpayne, where he was in the restaurant business servicing mining communities. My dad was born in Hearst, Ontario, because Hornpayne was so small and there was no hospital. They later moved to Toronto when Granddad retired in his early 70s. He lived in Toronto until he died in 1996 at 104 years of age.

— *Ciara, Grade 4, as told by her family*

My Uncle

One day my uncle was walking on a bridge. Suddenly he fell in to the lake. Then he went home in wet clothes.

The next day he was sick. My grandma saw my uncle lying on the bed, so my grandma went to get medicine.

At night, my grandma dreamed that my uncle stepped on a skull when he fell in the lake. In the morning, my grandma knew that a person who had died in the lake didn't forgive him, so she went to the place where my uncle fell. She brought fruit and she put the fruit on a plate. Then she kneeled down and begged that person not to make my uncle sick.

— *Anh, Grade 6*

The Water Ghost

A long time ago, back in my country when I was 2 or 3 years old, my dad was a fisherman. One day my dad went out onto the ocean with my 8th oldest uncle and my 10th oldest uncle. I don't know what they were doing, but they were not fishing. My dad was in the ocean doing something when a water ghost tried to drown him. A water ghost is a spirit of someone who died in the water. My uncle helped my dad and he survived.

— *Thinh, Grade 8*

From life story to drama

Tell students that they are going to use one of these heritage stories as a source for drama. In small groups, have them select one for dramatization. Ask them to consider these questions:

- Why do you think this story is important to the author?
- How will your group dramatize the story?
- How can you bring this incident to life and yet retain the story's original mood?
- How will you share the story? For example, will one of you be a storyteller while the others mime the action? Will all members of your group role-play the story?
- Who will speak the narrative in your group?
- Will you use dialogue?
- Where will movement fit into the telling of the story?
- How will your group involve all of its members?

What's your story?

In this phase of the work, your class can go through the same process as the group that originated the heritage presentations.

1. Tell the students something like this: "By yourself, decide on a family story. The event may have happened when you were younger or have happened recently. It could also be a story about something that happened to your parents or grandparents. Often, family get-togethers provide opportunities for hearing these kinds of stories."
2. Next, prompt the students to tell their stories to partners, and listen to their partners' stories. They then tell their stories to new partners and listen to their new partners' stories. Say: "Now tell the story that your partner told you, as if it had happened to you. You may have to make some minor adjustments. With your partner, clarify any details that were needed in the second telling of the story."
3. In small groups, students then tell their expanded stories, one member at a time. Each group selects one story that it would like to work on for the next

session. Say: "Using this story as the basis for your work, begin to investigate all of its drama potential." Prompt groups to consider these questions:

- What incidents could be dramatized?
- What roles will the members of the group play?
- How will the drama begin and end?
- Can you use mime, tableau, or movement along with your story? Could you use music?

4. The groups then share their stories with one another. Some groups may have been exploring the same story. If so, they can combine their efforts into one presentation.

5. As the stories are enriched and polished throughout the following sessions, they can become the basis for a class presentation. If this happens, help the students to consider questions such as the following:
   - Who will the audience be (another class in the school, parents in the community, a senior citizens' home)?
   - Will you arrange the audience in a circle with the players in the middle?
   - Will masks help set the context?
   - How will you open and close your presentation? Will you use music?

Extensions: (1) You may want to have these dramatized stories written down as scripts that can be made into a class booklet. (2) Perhaps your class could interview members of a particular community, such as one specific family or members of a club. These interviews could form the basis of a drama presentation to the original interviewees.

Exploring Character

A Grade 5 teacher who was exploring character motivation with her class used a drama convention known as role on the wall (see the Glossary, "Overview of Drama Conventions") in conjunction with the folk tale "The Honey Gatherer's Three Sons." The teacher specifically chose this technique because it helped her students gather, infer, analyze, and elaborate on the actions of characters in the story. Here is the story she shared.

The Honey Gatherer's Three Sons

A honey gatherer had three sons, all born at the same time. Their names were Hear-it-however-faint-the-sound, Follow-it-however-great-the-distance and Put-it-together-however-small-the-pieces. These names are sufficient to indicate the skill of these young men, but their friends simply called them Hear, Follow, and Piece.

One day the honey gatherer went on a long, long journey into the forest until he came to a tree that was as high as a hill, and the bees that buzzed in and out showed clearly that it must be full of honey. He climbed up, but, balancing on a rotten branch, fell to the ground and was broken into ten pieces.

Hear was sitting beside the hut in the village, but he promptly jumped to his feet, saying, "Father has fallen from a tree. Come! Let us go to his help."

His brother Follow set out and led them along the father's tracks until they came upon the body lying in ten pieces. Piece then put all the parts together, and fastened them up. Later, father then walked home while the sons carried his honey.

Next day, the honey gatherer again set out to look for honey, while his sons sat at home, each boasting that he was more important than the others.

"You could not have heard him without me," said Hear.

"Though you had heard him you could not have found him without me," said Follow.

"Even though you had found him, you could not have put him together without me," said Piece.

Meanwhile the old honey gatherer had gone far into the forest until he came to a tree that was as high as the clouds, and the bees buzzing in and out showed clearly that it must be full of honey. He climbed up, but he stepped on a rotten branch and it broke. The honey gatherer fell to the ground and was broken into a hundred pieces. His sons were sitting at home boasting about their individual skills, when Hear jumped up, saying, "Father has fallen!"

Follow reluctantly set out to follow the footprints, and found the hundred pieces on the ground. Pointing to them he said, "See how indispensable I am. I have found him for you."

Piece then put the hundred parts together very grudgingly, saying, "I, and I alone, have restored Father."

Their father walked home, while the sons carried the honey.

The next day the old honey gatherer went farther than ever into the forest and he found a tree that reached to the stars. The bees buzzing in and out showed that it must be full of honey. He climbed up, but treading on a rotten branch, fell to the ground and was broken into a thousand pieces.

Hear heard the fall, but would not tell his brothers. Follow knew that there must have been an accident since his father did not return, while Piece realized that his father needed his assistance, but would not condescend to ask his brothers to find him so that he might piece him together.

So the old honey gatherer died, because his selfish sons each thought more of his own reputation than of his father's. In truth, each needed the others, and none was wiser or better than the rest.

From *The Magic Drum: Tales from Central Africa* by W. F. P. Burton (New York: Criterion, 1962).

After the read-aloud, the teacher drew a rough sketch of a figure on the chalkboard to set up use of role on the wall. She asked the class which of the three sons they might like to speak with. After some discussion, Piece was the character chosen. Sticky notes were distributed to the students, and they were asked to jot down one word they would use to describe the character of Piece. One at a time, the students came up to the sketch and placed the sticky notes inside the figure.

Next, the teacher had the students write down a question they would ask Piece. They also had to jot down how they thought Piece might reply. These notes were posted around the sketch.

In the hot seat

The teacher read aloud the character descriptions and questions that had been posted, then asked for one volunteer to play Piece and two more volunteers to be Piece's mind in case the character needed help with answers to the questions. Piece was seated in a chair before the class and "the mind" sat behind. Students were then invited to question the character. During the lesson, several students were given the opportunity to play Piece and several others, his mind. In one instance, a student playing Piece was asked: "You knew your father was in difficulty, but you refused to let on. Does that make you a murderer?" The mind advised him not to answer the question. In another instance, Piece was asked, "Did you get along with your brothers when you were young?" The mind advised that there had been a lot of fighting.

Extension: Students in pairs interviewed each other. Many tried other roles such as the father and one or other of the two brothers.

A universal tale

At the conclusion, the teacher pointed out that traditional tales make good entertainment, but that in all cultures, the stories have a deeper purpose as well. She invited the students to give opinions on what they thought the story meant to the people who had created it and whether that meaning had purpose in the modern world.

Other Stories That Lend Themselves to Investigation

- "Cap-O-Rushes" in *English Fairy Tales* by Joseph Jacobs
- "Unananna and the Elephant" in *African Myths and Legends* by Kathleen Arnott
- "The Honest Penny" in *Little Book of Northern Tales: The Bear Says North* by Bob Barton
- "The Carpet of Dreams" in *Tales Told in Tents: Stories from Central Asia* by Sally Pomme Clayton

---

Entering the Story in Role

In the work with "The Honey Gatherer's Three Sons," students interviewed or hot-seated another student who was in role. The student in role tried to imagine the inner thoughts and feelings of the character and was supported by two other students playing the character's "mind."

Teacher-in-role

In the nursery rhyme "Tommy Trot," students can go beyond exploring interviews: the verse offers opportunities to build on the story and encourages creative responses within the context of that story. By having everyone working in role, the potential to generate greater understanding of story or plot is enhanced. The participation of the teacher-in-role creates opportunities for the drama to take a new direction or to be enlarged or extended beyond the original subject matter.

One teacher began the session by teaching students the verse "Tommy Trot" using an echoing strategy. He had students echo back each line after he spoke it. Next, two lines at a time were delivered and echoed back. Eventually, all four were given and echoed back at one time.

Tommy Trot

Tommy Trot, a man of law
Sold his bed and lay upon straw;
Sold the straw and lay on grass,
To buy his wife a looking glass.

Further chanting of the piece together involved adding a rhythm, exploring speed of delivery and volume, and creating a clapping game.

Developing the story

The teacher now turned the rhyme into a prose story, as follows.

> There was once a man named Tommy Trot. Tommy was a lawyer, a good one too, who defended many people in trouble at court. He worked very hard and was very successful at his job.
>
> Now it happened that Tommy had married a woman who was always wanting things: a new dining room table, a grandfather clock, a fountain for the garden, a bigger and better house. Whatever she asked for, Tommy agreed to. Now it really doesn't matter how much you earn if you spend faster than you earn it. Before he knew it, Tommy was deep in debt. Did his wife notice? Apparently not, for she just kept demanding more.
>
> Tommy sold the house and most of the furniture. The couple moved into the back of the barn.
>
> By this time, his wife had her eye on an antique looking glass that was supposed to have belonged to a Chinese emperor. It was encrusted in gold and the glass was encircled with diamonds. She had to have it. Well, she wheedled and whined and prodded and pushed until Tommy gave in. He sold the straw. He sold the barn, and they took up residence in a nearby meadow.
>
> Now when he appears in court, there are burrs on his jacket and grass stains on his trousers. As for his wife, she appears transfixed by the mirror and sits in the meadow staring into it all day long.

The teacher explained that the class was going to enter the story as hired laborers and that he was going to take some roles as well, first as a foreman, then as Tommy Trot, and later as Mrs. Trot. In order that the students would know which role he was playing at any given time, the teacher explained he would wear a hat as the foreman, wear a scarf as Tommy, and hold a hand mirror as Mrs. Trot. He also explained that when he took the items off and set them down he was no longer in role.

The teacher put on the hat and addressed the students.

> Good morning, everyone. Thanks for being on time. We have to remove all the straw from Tommy Trot's barn and load it onto these wagons. You'll earn good money if you work hard. Now, did you bring your tools? Show me what you've brought.

The teacher moved among the students, questioning them about their imaginary tools and asking for demonstrations of their use. Then he said, "Find a place

alone now and when I start telling the story of our job, you carry out the work."
He began speaking:

> One morning, a team of workers arrived at Tommy Trot's barn. They got
> out their rakes and started to rake and rake the straw into piles. When the
> piles were ready they took pitchforks and tossed the straw up into wagons.

The teacher stopped the drama, told the students the work was finished, and said,
"It's time to collect our pay. Let's knock on Tommy Trot's door."

The teacher removed the hat and the class discussed how they would go about
asking for their pay. Should they explain how hard they worked? Should they
show him examples of how well they had managed their tasks?

The teacher now put on a scarf, and the students summoned Tommy Trot. The
teacher-in-role went about as the students pointed out what they had accomplished, and in the end, Tommy thanked them and told them to return next week
for their pay.

At this juncture, the teacher came out of role and the class discussed their situation, asking these questions:

- Why aren't we getting paid?
- Can we ask to have the money sooner?
- If he doesn't have any money, can he borrow some?

The students wanted to knock on Tommy's door again and get some answers.

The teacher-in-role as Tommy was sympathetic and apologetic. Problem was
he was out of money until his next payday. He also explained that trying to pay
for his wife's extravagances was keeping him poor. "The antique mirror was the
last straw. I've nothing left!"

Finally, Tommy asked the students to speak to his wife and try to explain that
the couple had to get its spending under control.

Out of role, the teacher discussed a possible meeting with Mrs. Trot. Mostly
the class tried to figure out what their approach to her would be. "We can't just
force ourselves upon her and start firing questions," they agreed. "What do we
want her to tell us?"

The teacher went into role as Mrs. Trot. The students had decided to approach
their subject in a friendly manner, to get her talking about the beautiful mirror.
They would then perhaps bring up the subject of their unpaid wages in order to
shame her into thinking about others and not just herself.

The tipping point occurred when Mrs. Trot revealed her extreme loneliness
and unhappiness with her husband who worked all the time, even at the dinner
table. Slowly the situation was reversed as Mrs. Trot questioned the workers
about solutions to her dilemma.

The session ended with the students helping Mrs. Trot compose a letter to her
husband containing three important questions he needed to think about.

Developing a Character

Role is made up of two parts: the self and the other person that the student becomes. The "self" half of the role allows students to use their values and responses in the drama situation to understand what has happened. The "other person" half of the role gives them the safety of exploring ideas and situations quite different from their own lives. When students can balance the "self" part of the role with the "other" part of the role — what the text provides to work with — they can believe in the role that they are playing. Finding the heart of the role means that they will have created drama.

In developing a character, students have more givens than in a role-playing situation. Perhaps the gender, the age, the disposition, or the background will be predetermined by the content or the context for the text they are exploring.

In the poem "He Loved Overripe Fruits," James Berry draws upon his childhood in the Caribbean for his portrayal of an older man. Students can create their own characters who may reflect the man in the poem, but be developed by the explorations in the drama. Consider how to help them develop characteristics of elderly people without stereotyping them.

Exploring back story and future

1. Invite the students to reflect on the older people they know. What are their favorite memories of them? Are their aunts, uncles, grandparents, or great-grandparents still alive? What particular problems do they have at this time in their lives?

2. Prompt the students to read the poem from the board or chart, and in partners, they can decide who is speaking and to whom. They can then use these lines as the opening of a scene where they improvise the rest of the conversation.

He Loved Overripe Fruits

Hot sweaty body carrying treats
my Caribbean Grandpa came home
turned his pockets inside-out
and gave us runny, soft, sticky sweets.

Other times, the sweaty wet pockets
brought us bruised, overripe fruits
like bananas or blackberries

or sometimes, mangoes, plums
gineps*, naseberries**
or a tempting mixture of these.

Other times we knew how
to push, tussle, compete hard
to take off Grandpa's boots.

Not always, but often,
turned upside-down, the boots
carried small-change in them:
tipped out all round the floor,
as he smiled, seeing who got how much.

From *A Nest Full of Stars* by James Berry

* *Ginep* big-tree fruit, bunched like grapes: creamy flesh covers its stones.
** *Naseberry* sapodilla-plum: having sweet brown flesh.

3. *Projecting a Character's Fate:* Have students form new groups of four. What characters and events are suggested by the poem? Ask the students to discuss a background story that results in the grandfather being placed in a seniors' home.

4. *A Day in the Life of . . .:* Students can explore the experience of the character discussed in the poem by working backwards from a significant moment or turning point in that person's life to build the story that accounts for the event: a strategy called "A Day in the Life of . . ." They can work in groups

using role play to depict key moments that may have occurred within a 24-hour period of the character's life. The scenes can then run in chronological sequence to depict the events leading up to the dramatically significant moment.

5. *Improvising Family Roles:* Some groups of four will need to split in half and join other groups to create groups of six. Within each group, labels need to be written for the following characters: Mother, Father, Older Brother or Sister, the Young Person, and Grandfather (93 years old). Have each group fix the labels on five chairs placed in a circle. Each student takes a seat and the role assigned by the chair's label. The sixth person, the Controller, sits on a chair behind the mother.

   In this improvisation, the young person's family is moving away. The situation is a farewell supper to which the old person has been invited. During the meeting, the young person's intention is to suggest that the family take the elderly friend with them. Once the improvisation is under way, the Controller can signal the group to change roles. The Controller takes the mother's chair, the person to the left of the mother becomes the Controller, and everyone else moves one chair to the right. Continue with the drama. Roles remain with the chairs, not individuals. Keep working until everyone has taken on every role.

6. *In Role as Senior Citizens:* Now, in new groups, the students can improvise a scene in which the old person returns to a seniors' home, having left without notifying the manager to see a new 3D film, and describes the adventure to others in the home. They should pay attention to the way in which the others would respond to the story, particularly if they have always wanted to do something like the character did.

7. *Improvising a Delegation:* The students join up with another group. They improvise a scene in which the old person leads a delegation to the office of the director of the seniors' home in order to demand a regularly scheduled trip downtown. The director of the home is reluctant to agree because of the cost of the trip and the responsibility of the home for the safety of its elderly inhabitants.

Role play with the whole group

To start this improvisation, you can read out the following to the class:

Welcome to the first meeting of our newly established voluntary agency for helping the elderly. I have been appointed director of this agency. I understand that you have all seen our newspaper advertisement seeking volunteers. Who will go out into the community and help the elderly in their own homes? Exact details of the nature of help needed are not yet known. This is your job: to determine what can be done by this agency. Come up with your own plans for projects. I will be in my office when you have ideas to discuss.

Now, divide the class up into groups of four to six, and have them discuss ways of helping the elderly, such as home visiting and helping to carry out tasks the aged might find difficult; they can also discuss fund-raising schemes to aid the agency's work (e.g., sponsored walks, a yard sale, a part-time job). As groups present their ideas, you can challenge them with the concerns that arise from them.

Tell the groups that each member is responsible for preparing the case history of an elderly person, creating the name, personal history, financial status, health report, and so on.

The drama starts again when the group arrives at its second meeting. At this meeting, still in role as director, ask to hear some of the case histories and question students about their facts. Students then have to consider some of the problems posed. Ask, for example, "How would you deal with an old person found lying on the floor too weak to move? How would you make that person comfortable?" Have students in their groups practise what they would do in such an emergency.

Students can then take turns observing the other groups and see that the right amount of care is taken. Each group must be able to prove its concern and ability to deal with the situation.

The final problem that students have to tackle is also posed by the director. "It may be necessary at some time that some of you will have to persuade an old person to move into a residence for seniors. This is a very difficult subject to tackle. Does anyone feel capable of so doing? Those who feel capable can show the group how they would do this."

A volunteer can role-play an elderly person to whom the students must break the news, tactfully. This role-playing allows the students to show empathy and compassion as integral to the drama.

Assuming a public service role

In this lesson, the context for the improvisation is that class members are in role either as social workers making a film for high-school audiences about the concerns and problems of elderly people or as actors in the public service film. The students can work in small groups, with some role-playing actors in the film and others, social workers who are directing and producing the film. Each group selects one concern to represent in their portion of the film and completes a polished, collaboratively developed improvisation in a set time. When all the groups are ready, one group at a time observes the others' work. As the group watches, comments upon, and discusses the other scenes, the students need to remember that they are still in role as either social workers or actors.

Teaching Technique: Whole-Class Involvement in a Single Improvisation

New kinds of learning will happen when the whole class builds the improvised drama. Students will still be asking questions, making decisions, sharing ideas, and negotiating with one another, but they will have much more to listen and respond to, and, of course, much more feedback for their work will be available. The large number of people participating can add to the drama's excitement and tension.

The group decides on the most important or most interesting idea of the resource (e.g., a story or poem, a curriculum topic, a Tweet, or a contemporary issue from the news).

This idea becomes the first focus of the drama. This focus will change constantly as the situation in the drama changes and as students make choices and decisions as a class. New possibilities will open up as students participate and contribute. By exploring and expanding the ideas and suggestions, the class can build the drama co-operatively.

Sometimes, even in whole-group improvisation, the class will need to work in pairs or in small groups in order to complete a task and allow the whole-class drama to continue. For example, there may be several sides to an issue. Your class may want to stop the drama and explore various interpretations. Each pair or small group can present an idea, and the class can choose the one most suitable to continue with. Or, the group might decide to include the thoughts of several small groups and redirect the whole drama. At times you may have to negotiate the problems that have arisen out-of-role and then continue the drama when the members have accepted the compromise. At other times the disagreement between the groups may be a more interesting idea for the drama than finding a single solution.

Because there are so many participants, you may have to act as a moderator or director, and guide the drama along. In order to focus and extend their ideas, you may elicit other options from the groups. At times, you may even assume a role, questioning, clarifying students' actions, causing them to make decisions. By working inside the work, you can constantly assist the group in building powerful drama. This type of ensemble work has group dynamics as its mind and theatre as its heart.

8

Mining the Story for Riches

When a story is selected as the source for dramatic exploration, it should be seen as a starting point, with many possible discoveries lying within the text and the rich subtexts underneath. With a text, we can work with the lines on the surface, we can probe the spaces between the lines, and we can project beyond the lines in all directions. The demonstrations that follow will investigate some possibilities for using and discovering the rich ideas for drama that a story contains.

Finding the Hidden Stories

Students can be presented with a source, such as Kenneth Oppel's *Silverwing*, and, in role, make decisions about how to develop the ideas of the group, giving and accepting leadership, and contributing and discussing suggestions for building the drama. Their decisions are important to the development of the drama, and the classmates will be responsible for the effects of those decisions. In this way, the group will be creating the different aspects of the conflict that it will then work to solve.

The struggle to solve conflict is what gives drama its power. In this sense, conflict is the core of drama. It is not necessarily a physical struggle, such as a sword-fight between enemies. It may be what happens in a situation where a consensus has to be established within a group. It may be what happens between two groups as each group struggles to hold on to what it believes and values. Or, conflict may happen within an individual as the person tries to determine a direction that should be taken or a goal that should be achieved. Drama is about confronting and trying to solve problems.

Problems or difficulties arising during the drama work can be handled in different ways. Sometimes they can be worked through in role without stopping the action. At other times, the drama will have to be stopped and the difficulties sorted out through discussion. It is important that the group always works at focusing and directing the action, so that the drama can be a spontaneous response to these challenges. This kind of drama is referred to as story drama.

Preparing for the drama unit

The class can prepare to enter the milieu of *Silverwing* by role-playing the bats in a game that relies on lack of sight and permits the students to enter the drama work as creatures.

The teacher and the students can hang leaves, rattles, bells, or anything noisy from high strings running across the room. One player is chosen Bat Catcher; the rest are Bats. The room is darkened or the Bats can be blindfolded. The Catcher tiptoes about, trying to avoid making the strings rattle and giving away where he or she is. Bats move around constantly as quietly as they can among the strings of noisemakers and try to avoid getting caught. (Bat Catcher whispers in the ear of any Bat caught and takes the Bat off to the Bat Cave, anywhere outside the Bat area.) The game continues until all the players are in the Bat Cave. The first one caught is the next Bat Catcher.

Circle drama based on *Silverwing*

The teacher and her Grade 6 students in an inner-city school were working with copies of *Silverwing* by Kenneth Oppel, a fast-paced adventure fantasy, full of cliff-hanging action — a perfect book to share with these students. The teacher began by reading aloud to the class. Set in a fantasy world of a bat colony, the novel chronicles the perilous adventures of Shade, the runt of the Silverwing colony, who becomes separated from the others and must take a remarkable journey in order to rejoin them. Here is an excerpt.

> With a terrible shriek, forty owls plunged toward Tree Haven, fire burning in their claws. Shade saw Frieda and Bathsheba fling themselves clear as the owls hurled their sticks at the tree, flames leaping as they struck bark. It can't burn, Shade thought desperately. It's been hit by lightning and it can't burn again. But it did. Sparks caught on the tree's blackened armor, along the branches, up the trunk.
>
> He had to stop it. Before his mother could hold him back, he flung himself into the air and plunged toward a growing patch of flame. He battered it with spread wings, again and again, until it sputtered out. He could do this, he could put out the fires and save Tree Haven. He looked around frantically, and launched himself at another fire. From the corner of his eye he saw his mother and dozens of other bats surge from their hiding places in the forest and soar toward their beloved roost. His heart leaped.
>
> "Put out the flames!" came the cry. "Stop the fire!" But the owls were waiting for them, and beat them back with their wings as effortlessly as if they were drops of rain.

The class chose scenes from the novel, and students improvised the dialogue that would have occurred among the characters. They worked as a whole class, often in a circle, and different students took part during each scene. Because the book races along like an adventure film, there was great opportunity for developing the interactions between the characters.

Scene 1 — Judgment: Students volunteered to role-play the female bats that had to discipline Shade for endangering their entire colony with his antics. The dialogue took place in the circle, with the student playing Shade standing in the middle. As the female bats questioned him and tried to arrive at a just punishment, they revealed so much information they had absorbed from the teacher's reading of the text. In this scene and the ones that followed, the author's research — the bat lore and natural history — filled their talk, and strengthened the tension and drama of the moment. No one had told them to memorize the details from the novel; they were using them spontaneously to move the action along, to deepen their roles, filling the room with the wing beats of 25 Silverwing bats.

Scene 2 — Negotiation: There were five secondary students in the classroom one morning as part of their co-operative learning project. The older students became the owls, enemies of the bats. They had to be persuaded to leave the bats alone, to let them migrate to Hibernaculum, their new home. In one powerful moment, the bats determined that they had to know if they could trust these owls, and one Grade 6 student asked whether he could examine an owl pellet to see if the remains were bat or rat. The high-school boy as owl mimed the regurgitation of the object with such skill that the class gasped as the Grade 6 student took it in his hand. Of course, the pellet was imaginary, but he held it in his hand, looked at it, turned and pronounced, "Rat." The work continued.

Scene 3 — Storytelling: The stories of the bat history and culture were lost during the fire. The teacher asked the students to remember a tale and tell it so elders could memorize it. The stories they told were of births and deaths and dangers and victories and journeys. They were full of every detail one could imagine, drawn from the text, placed in the new context. And the students used the names the author had used — Greek and Latin names, and the biblical names of angels.

Recording Their Stories: The students wrote the stories that they had previously told aloud on dark purple paper with silver pens. One by one they read aloud their memories of the bat colony.

Teaching Technique: **Creating a Story Drama**

In a story drama, we translate the experience of the story that was used as a resource and shared as a class into opportunities for developing a drama unit, a series of lessons, each building on the previous ones, evolving into a strong created story.

Helpful prompts for structuring a story drama event

These statements and questions act as prompts for finding ways of rethinking and redirecting the work in progress. You may ask one student-in-role to clarify his or her position, or you may ask a group to replay what it has created so that the class can interpret their suggestions:

- *[Repeating their words]* Is that what you said?
- Is that what you meant?
- What are the implications of what you have said?
- What are the implications of what you have done?
- What do others think about their actions?
- Show me the effect of what she [or he] has said or done.
- Remind me of how this work began.
- Reminisce about your lives (in role) before this event began.
- What happened in the past that affected this action?
- Flash back to the incident . . .
- Flash forward to a future . . .
- Freeze the action so that we can see what is happening.
- Ask someone about an action or a statement you saw or witnessed.
- Talk aloud and all at once about your responses to what has happened.
- In groups, revisit and replay the scene where . . .
- Gather as a group to observe the scene where . . .
- With a partner, explore what happens when . . .
- Create a frozen picture of . . .
- Alone, create the scene where . . .
- In a circle, one by one, comment on the story so far.
- In groups, draw a diagram of . . .
- I will be working in role alongside you as . . .
- This is a story of a group of people who . . .

Extending the Story

First of all, the students need to meet the story through listening to the teacher read it aloud or by reading their own copies. After that, they can discuss it, and through conversation, share their subsequent questions and interpretations; these, in turn, can lead to a drama exploration where they develop and extend the *what if . . .* subtext generated by the original story.

Here is the text of a story that students can extend through use of various drama conventions and strategies that promote spontaneous improvisation.

The Swan Maiden

A young peasant, who often amused himself with hunting, saw one day three swans flying toward him, which settled down upon the strand of a sound nearby. Approaching the place, he was astonished at seeing the three swans divest themselves of their feathery attire, which they threw into the grass, and three maidens of dazzling beauty step forth and spring into the water.

After sporting in the waves awhile they returned to the land, where they resumed their former garb and shape and flew away in the same direction from which they came.

One of them, the youngest and fairest, had, in the meantime, smitten the young hunter that neither night nor day could he tear his thoughts from the bright image.

His mother, noticing that something was wrong with her son, and that the chase, which had formerly been his favorite pleasure, lost its attractions, asked him finally the cause of his melancholy, whereupon he related to her what he had seen, and declared that there was no longer any happiness in this life for him if he could not possess the fair swan-maiden.

"Nothing is easier," said the mother. "Go at sunset next Thursday evening to the place where you last saw her. When the three swans come give attention to where your chosen one lays her feathery garb, take it, and hasten away."

The young man listened to his mother's instructions, and, betaking himself, the following Thursday evening, to a convenient hiding place near the sound, he waited, with impatience, the coming of the swans. The sun was just sinking behind the trees when the young man's ears were greeted by a whizzing in the air, and the three swans settled down upon the beach, as on their former visit. As soon as they had laid off their swan attire they were again transformed into the most beautiful maidens, and, springing out upon the white sand, they were soon enjoying themselves in the water.

From his hiding place the young hunter had taken careful note of where his enchantress had laid her swan feathers. Stealing softly forth, he took them and returned to his place of concealment in the surrounding foliage.

Soon thereafter two of the swans were heard to fly away, but the third, in search of her clothes, discovered the young man, before whom, believing him responsible for their disappearance, she fell upon her knees and prayed that her swan attire might be returned to her. The hunter was, however, unwilling to yield the beautiful prize, and, casting a cloak around her shoulders, carried her home.

Preparations were soon made for a magnificent wedding, which took place in due form, and the young couple dwelt lovingly and contentedly together.

One Thursday evening, seven years later, the hunter related to his wife how he had sought and won her. He brought forth and showed her, also, the white swan feathers of her former days. No sooner were they placed in her hands than she was transformed once more into a swan, and instantly took flight through the open window.

In breathless astonishment, the man stared wildly after his rapidly vanishing wife, and before a year and a day had passed, he was laid, with his longings and sorrows, in his allotted place in the village churchyard.

Once the students know the story, they can begin to wonder about its implications and consider its untold aspects. They can extend the background, the lives of the characters, the unexplained events, and the *what if . . .* moments that fill the reader's imagination.

Ways to extend the story

See the Glossary, "Overview of Drama Conventions," for a summary of common drama conventions.

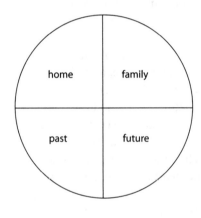

Here are a variety of drama conventions or strategies that can assist students in their wonderings about and their wanderings through the text.

Circle of Life: Aspects of the life of the swan maiden's husband can be represented in four sections of a circle on a large sheet of paper: (1) Home, (2) Family, (3) Past, and (4) Future. The class can be divided into four groups to brainstorm the incidents and information about each of the categories, building up a composite picture from the minimal information offered in the story. These descriptions can form the basis for improvised dialogue between the husband and one other person from the category. For example, the husband could have a conversation with his own father about his upcoming marriage.

Inner and Outer Circle: The class can form two circles, one within the other. The outer circle represents the husband; the inner one represents the wife. The two characters express their own viewpoints of their behaviors, one player at a time. A volunteer in the outer circle as the husband begins speaking, and then a player in the inner circle replies as the wife. Players can add their voices as they wish in a variety of roles, perhaps as eavesdroppers, friends, or sages. Students-in-role can describe their reactions and thoughts about the happenings in the story. The outer circle can rotate, and activities can be repeated (sometimes with new prompts) so students can further experience a variety of points of view or deepen their learning.

Collective Character: The entire class works together to represent the nature of the husband. As the students take turns in speaking his thoughts and words, the character's nature will alter, and students will begin to understand the composite picture they are creating.

Objects of Character: Items can be brought in (or drawn) to flesh out the character in the drama. The objects or possessions can raise questions for the group whose task is to interpret how they fit into the character's life. The teacher can provide the items, or the students can present them as artifacts necessary to the building of the drama. For example, what did the wife bring to the marriage home inside the large silk scarf she hid under the bed?

If I Were You . . . : Different students can approach the husband, put a hand on his shoulder, and complete the sentence "If I were you . . ." In this way, advice is given to help the husband to make a decision: perhaps he didn't die, but decided to marry again. Advice can be given in role or out of role. As the students act out their suggestions, it may help if traditional Japanese music is played quietly.

Teaching Technique: Spontaneous Improvisation

Students are given information for beginning the drama, but group members are responsible for the direction the drama takes. No answers are provided, and it is understood that there are no right or wrong endings. Students can find clues in the starting points given, but they need to suggest directions and build on the ideas of others. The action in spontaneous improvisation is open-ended. It is the process of improvising that helps develop drama skills, not the product created.

Once the drama begins, the group has the responsibility for maintaining the improvisation. Members will explore situations in a game-like atmosphere, learning the give-and-take of improvisation, free from a critical audience, and concerned with maintaining the improvisation, solving problems, and making decisions. This is the excitement of working in improvised drama — students initiate the action, develop the drama spontaneously, and then face the consequences of their actions.

In a prepared improvisation, however, the group has an opportunity to replay the event, change roles, clarify the process, and determine how it will be seen by others. These prepared improvisations can then be used in exploring the theme or the context as the drama is developed.

Delving for Deeper Meanings

A Short Short Story

The last man on Earth sat at his desk. Suddenly he heard a knock at the door.

This brief science-fiction story has many explanations that the students can brainstorm. It can be motivating to see how many reasons for "the knock" that they can discover. Be sure to permit no repetitions of categories (only one robot, one creature). One Grade 7 class generated this list:

the wind, a meteorite, an earthquake, a woman, a child, God saying that it is time to go, a BlackBerry timer going off, the devil ready for his soul, a raccoon, a tree branch, his heartbeat, the Internet, his imagination, a zombie, a robot, an alien, his dream, an angel, his own spirit returning, an object that fell off his desk

Creating a parallel universe

Rather than dramatizing this story, the students can begin to build their own story drama using elements of the sci-fi story. By selecting a parallel universe, they can create a people or inhabitants whose existence resulted in there eventually being one man left on Earth. You can provide instructions such as these:

1. *Gathering Information:* Ask students working in groups to explore one aspect of the life of the chosen people, such as clothing, education, family, food, health, law, leisure, shelter, travel, war, work, or worship. Each of these

aspects can be broadened or made specific. For example, if food is the topic that the group chooses to explore, members can demonstrate how food is found — fishing, hunting, trapping, gathering; who finds the food; and who distributes the food.

When students are ready to share their work, they can present their improvisations to the class group by group. Those watching can then comment on what they understood about their demonstrations. This sharing can prepare the students for the next phase of the activity: to develop a ritual that the imagined people would have carried out.

2. *Using Rituals:* Advise students that all peoples have certain rituals to help them mark the stages in life. Marriage is one example. You could say, "If examining the rites of marriage in your clan, you might create the text of a wedding ceremony and use various properties, such as a ring, rice, confetti, veil, and white dress. You might stage a tableau which shows what the ritual stands for. For example, it could celebrate a couple's commitment, formalize their commitment, provide public acknowledgment and acceptance of the couple's commitment, legalize the contract or serve as a religious rite, and fulfill cultural and role expectations."

Similarly, using various improvisational techniques, students can examine the rituals associated with birth, coming to maturity, setting out on a journey, or homecoming.

Challenge students working in groups with the following:

In your group, choose and develop your ritual. How can you develop ways of drawing the rest of the class into your work without having lengthy out-of-role directions and instructions? For example, most cultures have some rituals where the "initiate" does not know what will be expected of him or her during the ceremony: the rites have been kept secret to protect the power of the ritual. So now it is your group's turn to initiate the others into the ritual. In this way, your audience is in role as members of your people.

3. *Storytelling Through Movement:* Have the class work in groups. Within each group, students discuss the fact that their people were visited by something long ago. If not human, what could the visitors have been? What effect did the visitors have on their tribe? Did they leave a legacy? Did they influence the way in which the tribe lived? Using only movement, each group tells the story of what happened long ago. When satisfied with the story being told, members plan how three or four tableaux that represent the story could be "painted" on temple walls.

When a group is ready with its tableaux, members present the frozen scenes. The audience observes the actors closely to learn as much as possible about the inhabitants. After the observing group has studied the scene, the class has a discussion so that the groups are clear about what is being depicted. Now, using movement, the group that last shared its scenes presents its story a second time. This time the students who were observers become an *involved* audience, portraying the visitors who discover the world. Then the groups can reverse the sharing and the involvement process.

4. Now the class can create their collaborative play drawn from the short story. Members will have to agree on how and why this one man was the last human on Earth or determine what that means within the drama. Perhaps the versions demonstrated by each group will reveal that, like much of history, the truth remains obscured.

Creating Parallel Stories

We may begin with one particular story with a class, but the students find a dozen more, some hidden in the recesses of their story minds, some discovered in the library, some evolved from storytelling sessions, and others created collaboratively through story-building activities. As teachers, we also add our own selections, some to be read or told aloud, others to be left on a table to be read by volunteers. One story gives birth to a thousand.

As we journey along story pathways, we may suddenly find a story we passed just recently reappearing with new life and new vitality (stories connecting stories, and stories being re-created).

Setting the context for playmaking

In the poetic novel *Ann and Seamus* by Kevin Major, we find the story of a ship bringing Irish immigrants to North America. In rough seas, the ship founders, and the passengers and crew scramble onto outlying rocks. They are rescued by a young woman, Ann, with her father and brother, who row them, a few at a time, to safety in Newfoundland.

This story became the scenario for a drama unit concerning the relationship of Ann and a young Irish man, Seamus, who had been saved by this courageous family.

The teacher of a Grade 7 class read the following poem from the novel that sets the scene for the story:

The story that surges from them
is a grievous, horrific tale
even for this stretch of coast.

Vessel: the brig Despatch
Captain: William Lancaster
Port of registration: Workington, England
Port of embarkation: Londonderry, Ireland
Date: 29th day of May 1828
Destination: Quebec City

These are the barest facts.
They tell us nothing of the misery and pain.
Woe are those who came into the hellish clutches
of Isle aux Morts.
Never was this home of ours better named.

In preparation for the drama, three students did a research project on the vessels that carried the Irish immigrants to their new homes. They shared their information, gleaned from Internet sites, in a seminar with the class. The ensuing discussion revealed many fascinating and significant details about the perilous journeys.

To begin the lesson, the teacher grouped the students in inner and outer circles: those on the inside told their reasons for leaving Ireland, while those on the outside shared their motivations for remaining in Ireland. They told each other their stories, strengthened by the research they had shared.

The teacher then read aloud the poem "Ann," and the students interviewed her in role as Ann. Their questions deepened their understanding of the time Ann's family moved to Newfoundland from the "old land," and other students clarified some of the questions and answers to fit the context of the drama.

Ann

I Dream of Books,
of reading and writing.

What father knows is fish.
For books he has no mind or heart.
Mother the same.
What learning's here is fish.

But the fish merchant's sons have their learning
or how would they grow
to be merchants like their father?
Their daughters the same.
They have their books.

In St. John's schoolhouse hold hundreds.
In Boston even more,
the Yankee trader said it's true.

But we are so few and distant
no teacher will come live among us.

Next, three students, who had read and prepared the poem "The Rescue," within *Ann and Seamus*, read the words aloud in role as the father, the brother, and Ann as narrator. The class set up a scene with the passengers stranded on the rocks, calling to the three in the boat to rescue them. The students made no sounds but mouthed their cries as the three in the boat stared, and in slow motion, threw a large rope to the stranded victims, who were then pulled one by one to the boat.

The Rescue

A wreck, no mistake, he says,
and our only course
to search for the hapless souls
who might survive these seas.

Ann, it'll not be easy.
the good lord will be with us.
The wind and weather against.

Father pats the head of a Hairyman
our dog, yelping his consent.

And what of me? says Tom.
I'm plenty man for the job.
I'll not be left behind.

Mother beholds her family
her worry buried in silence,
buried with her fear of the seas
as eager to swallow one of us
as give up any we might rescue.

In the next scene, the villagers comforted the passengers, in pairs, and asked questions about their hopes for the future. The teacher simply pointed to each pair to continue speaking, and the rest of the class remained silent while they listened.

Then, a student-in-role as Seamus read the poem titled after the character to the class. The student had prepared the poem in advance. The rest of the class questioned him about his intentions to travel to America rather than remaining in Newfoundland. Much of the history revealed in the previous seminar provided information for the role players.

Seamus

From county Donegal I come.
Seamus Ryan is the name I carry
across the Atlantic, where I will make
for myself another life.

My Ireland is no place for
a man of eighteen years,
his family driven into the soil
by taxes and damnable landlord.

Strong backs are needed in Quebec
and in Baltimore and New York I hear.
I might not tarry long
once my feet touch land.
I'll turn south to America,
as far away from the vile of English
as I can get.

The teacher explained that Ann had a life-altering decision to make. She and Seamus developed a relationship. On the day when Seamus was preparing to leave with the others who had been rescued, Ann had to decide whether to remain or leave with him. The students had not yet read the novel, and the decision was not predetermined. They sat at tables of four, in role as the families of villagers, and discussed Ann's situation until they had determined in their groups whether she should go or stay. One member at the table was asked to present the significant reason behind the group's decision, while one student as Ann stood in the centre, listening to each position. Ann then announced her intention to stay or leave — in this class, she chose to remain in Newfoundland.

The teacher revealed that this story was based on a real person named Ann Harvey, who had rescued these stranded passengers, and her decision also was to remain. The class then silently read the poem "Cod" before creating together a choral presentation to complete the unit of drama.

Cod

is all the reason in the world
to settle in this cove

Cod
fills our boat,
thick and lusty fish
some days in the swarms as dense as fog.

Cod
to gut and split abroad
and wash and salt and spread
outdoors upon the rocks
to stack and store and spread again.

This, the reason we are on this earth —
to turn cod into dried salt cod
for the tables of the world?

The teacher placed a copy of the book in the classroom library to be read by those who wanted to explore the other aspects of the story. The class had developed its own parallel story, and by coincidence, constructed a similar ending.

Teaching Technique: **Adding Tension to the Drama**

Tension can be created through *the secret, the mystery, the surprise, the dangling carrot, the time frame,* and *the space limit.* Teachers need to incorporate dramatic pressures so that the students engaged in the drama will know the complexities of the situation they are facing. We have to be careful that the added tension will add to the drama, not just be a burden to their work. These pressures can deepen their responses in the drama.

- We can introduce a surprising or shocking experience into the drama. For example, we can foreshadow that one of the people in the great canoe will die. The shock may force the students into rethinking what they were going to do.
- We can pull the experience in the opposite direction to where it seems to be going. In a plan where the class in role were to take over a community by appearing in the early morning fog, we tell them the fog has disappeared, the sky is clear, and we are in view of the enemy village.
- We can insist that they speak in a way that the king will accept, using carefully chosen language registers to influence him.
- We can place special demands on the role players: they will have to solve a riddle, only one person knows the combination for the safe, or the swans will return earlier than normal because of the eclipse of the sun.
- We can add an emotional constraint (one role player is embarrassed or is planning to leave the family).

- We can move the drama to a different space, either in the fictional design of the dramatic space (in a locked room) or in a different actual space (a large stairwell).
- We can also ask students to become the experts in a field (those who have information on a particular animal almost extinct, or those who understand a people's culture on an island we are about to visit).
- One of the most effective tensions is to slow down the work deliberately by asking the students to reflect within the drama on what has happened. For example, students may see three plans enacted in order to choose only one: (1) they can rehearse the battle with the monster to check the state of their weapons; (2) they can use a flashback or a flash-forward to heighten the choices they must make; and (3) they can be required to do careful planning exercises using chart paper and markers.

Unpacking the Story

Charles Causley's poem "What Has Happened to Lulu?" appears simple and straightforward, but its series of short, sharp questions creates a feeling of tension and anxiety. The sudden disappearance of Lulu is a mystery that generates much interest and discussion with students. Why did she leave? What happened to her? Where did she go? What did she write in her note?

Because the poem gives only the sketchiest of details, drama activities can help students to develop their own ideas about the story and expand upon them, to explore characters and relationships, and to investigate multiple viewpoints.

Four dramatic ways to work with the poem

Work with the poem in classrooms has involved drama in the following ways.

1. *Script Writing:* In one class, students working in groups of three were assigned one stanza of the poem and asked to turn it into a script. The teacher reviewed desired script components (stage directions placed before speeches; names of speakers shown to the left; notations about how each speaker speaks, such as cheerfully or angrily, and how the speaker moves, such as pacing the floor). In each scene, the student playing Lulu's mom was to mime the part. The remaining lines were to be spoken between the other two students. Each scene was to begin and end with a still image.
    Sample script for stanza 6:

    > Mom moves across Lulu's bedroom towards the door. Both students follow on her heels.
    > **Lauren:** (tearful voice, upset, reaches for Mom's elbow) Why do you wander about as though . . .
    > **David:** (frustrated, angry voice, darts in front of Mom) . . . you don't know what to do? What has happened to Lulu, mother?
    > **Lauren:** (bursting into tears) What has happened to Lu?

    When the scenes had been rehearsed, the teacher gathered the class into a carousel, or circle for sharing the work. In a carousel, groups are ordered in number of presentation, and everyone remains still and silent until it is their group's turn to share. The work can be enhanced by requesting each group to begin with a still image, to be held for a slow count of five, and to end with another still image, held for the same duration. Music, appropriate to the subject matter being explored, can further enhance the work. In this case, the scenes were played in order, the class gaining a strong visual sense of the world of the poem.

2. *Working in Collective Role:* In another class, the teacher used a collective role strategy to build information about Lulu, her family, and her community. The students were divided into four groups. Each group was given a role. Group 1 represented Lulu's homeroom teacher. Group 2 played Lulu's mom. Group 3 played Lulu's younger sibling. Group 4 took the role of next-door neighbor.

   The teacher explained that she would take the role of an interviewer, and when she approached a group and asked a question, any one group member or as many members as wanted to could answer. The teacher requested that the students listen carefully to the responses of others so that some consistency within group roles could be maintained.

   The teacher then approached a group, posed a question, improvised with the students on their answers, and then went to another group. By her moving back and forth among the groups, building on leads and making connections, a detailed story of Lulu's life began to emerge.

   Sample questions to the neighbors:
   - How long have you known the family?
   - What are they like as neighbors?
   - Do Lulu's friends come around?
   - Have you noticed any changes in Lulu's habits of late?

   Sample questions to Lulu's mom:
   - Can you give me a physical description of your daughter?
   - What two words sum up your daughter's personality?
   - When Lulu has problems, whom does she turn to?
   - What problems are you and Lulu experiencing at home?

   Sample questions to Lulu's homeroom teacher:
   - What kind of student is Lulu?
   - Is she having any problems with her peers?
   - Have her parents expressed any concerns?
   - Has she ever confided in you?

   Sample questions to Lulu's younger sibling:
   - Can you tell me some of Lulu's favorite pastimes?
   - What is your relationship like with her?
   - If Lulu could change anything at home, what do you think that would be?
   - If you could give her a gift to make her happy, what would you choose?

3. *Mime and Note Writing:* In a sequence of lessons, a class of nine- and ten-year-olds silently enacted scenes from the poem through mime and tableaux. These included a scene in which Lulu, a runaway teenager, jumped into a waiting car on the night of her disappearance and a scene about the discovery and reading of Lulu's note to her mother. The teacher noticed that these opportunities to enact the text generated bursts of writing as students decided what would be in their scene.

Then, moving from enactment into writing, students quickly wrote what they thought might appear in Lulu's farewell note to her mother and crumpled the message as described in the poem. The teacher described what happened:

> After the drama there was an intense period of writing, very short and silent. I didn't even ask for silence, all I said to them was: remember, this is a note that made your mother cry.

For these students, the poem had become real, they were involved in it, and they were taking part in it through their enactment and their writing.

4. *Digital Drama:* One teacher set up an Internet account and the students in role as family, friends, or neighbors wrote emails to Lulu (the teacher-in-role). Through the miracles of the Internet, Lulu replied to them directly and explained why she had felt the need to run away.

> Dear Lulu,
> Where have you gone? I saw you climb out your window at night a week ago. I tried to follow you, but you just disappeared in the night. Are you ever going to come back? My daughter misses you coming over. Please be in a safe area and please come back.
>
> Your neighbour

> Dear Lulu,
> Me and Mom are worried sick! Where are you? Why did you leave us? I have so many questions to ask you. I hope you're safe. We saw that your money box was gone. Did you decide to run away because of us? Please write back.
>
> Sincerely,
> Your brother

> Dear Lulu,
> I miss you dearly. This is your Brother. I want to let you know since you left the house has been dull and boring. I know you used to tease me but I still would like you to come home. Life was and is still miserable. Lulu if you're out there please come home.
>
> Brother

Taking the drama to the Internet was an enticement for many students to write more than usual. The teacher noted that many students kept up a correspondence with Lulu, and in so doing, both the story and the lengths of their correspondence grew.

Here is the poem that occasioned all of this dramatic activity.

What Has Happened to Lulu?

What has happened to Lulu, mother?
    What has happened to Lu?
There's nothing in her bed but an old rag-doll
    And by its side a shoe.

Why is her window wide, mother,
    The curtain flapping free,
And only a circle on the dusty shelf
    Where her money-box used to be?

Why do you turn your head, mother,
    And why do the tear-drops fall?
And why do you crumple that note on the fire
    And say it is nothing at all?

I woke to voices late last night,
    I heard an engine roar.
Why do you tell me the things I heard
    Were a dream and nothing more?

I heard somebody cry, mother,
    In anger or in pain,
But now I ask you why, mother,
    You say it was a gust of rain.

Why do you wander about as though
    You don't know what to do?
What has happened to Lulu, mother?
    What has happened to Lu?

— *Charles Causley*

9

Researchers and Role Players

Students as experts can create a drama event that involves them in using their research skills and locating significant information to add to their improvised work. By surrounding a drama work which was stimulated by a fictional story with information, students are combining fiction and fact to create their own narratives. Researching a topic can involve exploring such factual resources as the Internet, blogs, interviews, letters, stories, and primary source documents. Students can gather all of the information with a view to gradually building a drama with the story work as the heart of the action. By engaging in inquiries to complement the drama, students are wearing the Mantle of the Expert, employing their knowledge and understanding as part of their roles.

Authorities on the Story

The following story about the Dust Bowl in the Prairies takes place in the 1980s and reflects similar conditions to the Dirty Thirties in North America. Fiction writers often use information carefully researched to ground the reality of their narratives. The story can begin a unit of study on those difficult conditions and incorporate the students as researchers as they locate information of all kinds to use in building their discussion, role-playing, and reading and writing experiences. Gathering a supply of resources allows the students to become researchers, collecting and organizing data to use as part of their theme building. If there is a library in the school, or if the public library is near, you can build your resource collection with books focusing on these times, such as *Out of the Dust* by Karen Hesse and *Children of the Great Depression* by Russell Freedman.

The Internet is such a valuable resource for building drama around information. Content on the Dust Bowl, such as the excerpt below, is readily available from Wikipedia, but the students are capable of searching for relevant facts, readily available on a variety of web sites.

> On April 14, 1935, known as "Black Sunday," twenty of the worst "Black Blizzards" occurred throughout the Dust Bowl, causing extensive damage and turning the day to night; witnesses reported that they could not see five feet in front of them at certain points.

Developing scenarios from history involves all the languaging processes for students of every age. They can read or listen to the story, and then begin to select incidents or situations with which to build an improvised scene. The data they have researched can inform and offer authenticity to their work. The text used in this lesson is from a picture book in which a boy, worried about losing the family farm to dryness in the 1980s, hears about his grandparents' fight to keep the farm in the Great Depression. His grandfather tells him:

"The dirt and the dust were everywhere. Your grandma stuffed towels in the crack at the bottom of the door to keep the dust out. When I went outside, I had to put a dish towel soaked in water over my nose and mouth. The dust drifted like snow against our fences, and even buried them sometimes. Students had to walk to school backwards to keep the wind-blown soil from stinging their faces. And when they got home, they had to clean the dust out of the nostrils of the cattle.

"And, oh, the dust clouds. How I remember them. Brown ones, red ones, yellow ones, made from the, soil of thousands of farms across the prairies. One big dust cloud blocked out the sun for days. As it moved across the country it covered the land in darkness. We had to keep the lanterns lighted all day. Some people in the cities thought the end of the world had come."

The following ideas are drawn from interpreting the story, remaking it into students' own construction. These are simply suggestions or prompts for initiating role play or improvised conversations. The drama is developed from the sub-text of the lines in the story, which serve as jumping-off points. Because of their researched preparation, the students can own the dialogue and the created drama by sharing their knowledge in small vignettes drawn from the story. The drama will accumulate and build because of their background as experts.

Guiding improvisations

Here is a suggested beginning for structuring improvised action. The italicized type represents questions asked or ideas shared by the teacher. Once the students have read the story, and the student-researchers have determined the historical data found in the references, you can lead them through a series of guided improvisations. Questions such as the following can be used as prompts to stimulate action and dialogue as students work out their responses. Sometimes, they will work with a partner or a small group, and sometimes as an ensemble, with individual students responding in role to the prompts.

The scenes that students will improvise will be strengthened by the bits of factual information that the students weave into their improvised responses to the prompts. The drama is thereby allowed to move into *felt* knowledge, where the characters are enriched by the facts brought to life surrounding their actions. This type of guided lesson, where you as teacher lead the students through a dramatization, scene by scene, can help students discover the various techniques used in drama: techniques comparable to the paint palette of the artist.

The full text for "The Dust Bowl" appears in Appendix C on pages 146 to 148.

1   From the sideboard, the pictures of his mother and his grandma smiled at him.

What were these two women saying to him from behind the pictures? Students can work in partners to evoke the words of the two women. How will details of the Dust Bowl be worked in? After they have had time to rehearse, select a few pairs to voice their thoughts in role. The boys may want to be the men of the house, repeating what the women were saying, as if the breezes were carrying their words to them.

2   When his father and his grandpa joined him at the table, they didn't say much, but he [Matthew] knew what they were thinking. Finally, he blurted out, "We aren't going to sell the farm, are we?"

What is each of the three characters sitting at the table thinking, but not saying?
You can use three volunteers at a time, with an alter ego standing behind each one of them, advising and whispering words that will help the characters to speak the thoughts of the three males. Then the roles can be changed with different students.

3   His grandpa stood up and walked over to the window. "The rain will come. The wheat will grow. It's not as bad as the last drought."

What was worse about the drought of the 1930s? Use the research the students have found. Could the information be heard on the radio as a soundscape?
Students can read their research items as newscasters, seated at a table. Setting the scene in the 1930s, they can add some banter back and forth as the reports are given.

4   "When your grandma and I first farmed this land, we were young. We thought we had discovered gold in those fields of waving wheat. The world needed wheat, and we wanted to grow enough of it for everyone.

How did Matthew's grandfather persuade his new wife to move out west to farm?
The scene can be dramatized in partners, and if the students want to role-play only same-sex roles, the sister or brother can be told about the persuasive conversation by the bride or bridegroom.

5   "We ploughed up all our land, even the field that we had decided not to seed yet. We borrowed from the bank and bought new equipment so we could plant as much wheat as possible. The prairies became a one-crop country.

In groups of three or four, have the students dramatize the interview between the bank manager(s) and the couple that needs a loan to continue.

6   "We needed luck, and the first year we found it. All the farmers did. The sun shone when it was supposed to, there was enough rain, the pests stayed away and the frost was late. Matthew, the prairies were covered with wheat.

The students can improvise the potluck dinner through creating a tableau where the farmers and their wives are talking about the good fortune that lies ahead in their lives. The teacher can bring snapshots from the tableau to life for a few seconds so the group hears snippets of the various conversations.

7   "Then the rain stopped completely and times got worse. A hot sucking wind began to feed on the bare soil, and it blew the earth away. The grass that had fed the buffalo for centuries was no more.

"That wind blew for two solid weeks, blowing from the four corners of the world, blowing the land out from under our feet. It was the Big Dry. You had to see it to believe it, Matthew. It turned our world into a dust bowl. It blew open doors, broke windows and even flattened a barn or two.

What questions did Matthew have about the Big Dry that his grandparents had lived through? What would his grandmother have told him about the past drought if she were there sitting in the rocker? Either you or a volunteer can role-play the grandmother while students ask questions as the children of this time.

8   "The dirt and the dust were everywhere. Your grandma stuffed towels in the crack at the bottom of the door to keep the dust out. When I went outside, I had to put a dish towel soaked in water over my nose and mouth. The dust drifted like snow against our fences, and even buried them sometimes. Students had to walk to school backwards to keep the wind-blown soil from stinging their faces. And when they got home, they had to clean the dust out of the nostrils of the cattle.

Groups of students could be the children talking to new classmates about their difficulties living through the Big Dry after they had moved west to California.

9   "And, oh, the dust clouds. How I remember them. Brown ones, red ones, yellow ones, made from the soil of thousands of farms across the prairies. One big dust cloud blocked out the sun for days. As it moved across the country it covered the land in darkness. We had to keep the lanterns lighted all day. Some people in the cities thought the end of the world had come.

In partners, back to back, one student from the city, the other from the farms, discuss the daylight darkness, not really hearing each other.

10   "Another cloud covered us — grasshoppers. They could black out the sun. Millions of them would stop all at once on a farm. They ate a crop in minutes, devouring every scrap of greenness. They even ate the bristles on the broom and the halter on the horse. When a train tried to run on tracks covered with grasshoppers, the wheels could get no traction, and they just spun around. Those insects could stop a train.

Everyone is in role at the church service when they turn and see the grasshopper army approaching, and volunteers predict the disasters that may follow.

11   "When many of my friends heard stories about the lush pickings on the west coast, they quit their farms. Tough farmers though they were, they left with their wives and kids, drained by heat and wind and cold and hardship. Chickens and everything else they owned were tied on the backs of the jalopies. Families were on the move. Schools were closed. The buildings were abandoned for good."

In teams of four, one couple is saying goodbye to those who will stay.

12   Matthew went outside. His father put down the hoe, climbed the steps and sat beside him on the porch. They both stared at the bluest of skies. "I love this farm, Matthew. Your mother loved it too. She was afraid to live here at first, afraid of the space and all the quiet. But when she planted her garden, she became a part of this farm. She belonged here. You do too."

Students work in groups of three or four: father, son, and behind them, mother (and grandmother) who is telling them whether they should stay on the farm or leave.

Reflecting on the drama experience

As a way of drawing the work to a close, have students read the words of the Woody Guthrie song "This Land Is Your Land," which is readily available. The song pictures the lives of those who were unemployed and who wandered the country searching for any kind of work or handouts. Students can sing in order to bring the words to life. One Grade 6 teacher played his guitar and sang a version of the song with the students joining in for a second playing.

A Novel Approach to Drama

Using a novel written for young people offers you a collection of connected sources for drama work. The ideas, the themes, the incidents, and the characters can act as contexts for drama. The story can be read aloud by the teacher or silently by the class; alternatively, it can simply act as a resource for the teacher to draw upon in planning a series of interconnected lessons. Students can create a parallel narrative, expand upon the story's inferred incidents, or dramatize events from the text.

The following unit is based on the historical novel *Trouble on the Voyage.* Jeremy, a homesick 11-year-old, finds himself serving as ship's boy with Captain Thomas James during his search for the Northwest Passage in 1631. Against a backdrop of harsh circumstances, Jeremy struggles to gain friends, learn responsibility, and deal with estrangement from his brother, Will, who is also aboard. Most of the story takes place in the bleak, frozen areas around Hudson and James bays. Themes explored include parenting, loss, learning and changing, safety and trust.

Thinking about the genre in role

1. Arrange some students in an inner circle facing out, and around this circle, have an outer circle facing in. Have the students adjust themselves so they are standing opposite a partner.
2. Pose this question: "What are some characteristics of sea adventures that appeal to all ages?" Students discuss with partners for one minute. Then students in the outer ring take one step to the left and begin the discussion with a new partner. Repeat three or four times to ensure that students are getting lots of ideas.
3. Now, have the students move to a new partner and determine who will be A and who, B. Student A goes into role as a professor of English giving a

lecture on why sea adventures appeal to all ages. Student B goes into role as a student in the professor's class. His focus is to interrupt the lecture to ask questions about the topic. Allow one minute for the activity, then have students A and B switch roles and play again.

4. Move among the participants, stopping the activity and interviewing professors or students about information they are imparting or questions they are asking.

Giving words and shape to the senses

1. Read the May 18, 1631, entry from Bob Barton's novel to the class (see text below). In this piece, Jeremy has an interview with the Captain and learns more about the mission. He is disappointed to learn he might be away two years. There is also a glimpse of the Lieutenant's bullying.

2. Create a class mind map of what Jeremy can see, hear, feel, and smell at this point in the voyage.

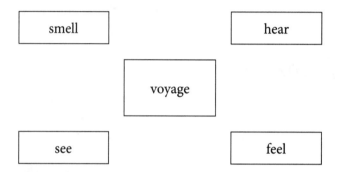

3. (a) Have students choose one aspect (e.g., how Jeremy feels) and elaborate on the language. For example: Jeremy is afraid of the Lieutenant.
   (b) Ask students to come up with words that convey a concrete description of what Jeremy is experiencing. The example "Jeremy is afraid of the Lieutenant" might become "The sight of the Lieutenant caused a numb feeling in his chest, and his legs weakened."

4. Now have the students in small groups try similar examples for the other senses. Reconvene the class. Share and record the samples.

5. (a) Ask the class to break into groups of three. Each group is to select one phrase from the list the class has generated.
   (b) Each group works out a way of chanting the phrase of interest and inventing a movement motif to accompany it. For example, while chanting "His stomach tightened; his knees were weak . . .," group members tighten their stomach muscles and then bend at the knees.

6. (a) Move the groups into a carousel and have each group form an opening still.
   (b) In role as the Lieutenant, move past each group focused on demonstrating Jeremy's feelings. As you do so, members should chant and move, freezing again once you in role as the Lieutenant have passed.
   (c) Experiment with different arrangements of the groups in the carousel.

7. Discuss possible situations the students think could occur in future entries on Jeremy and the Lieutenant or the Lieutenant and Jeremy's brother, Will.

Trouble on the Voyage: May 18, 1631

I haven't seen much of the Captain since we left England. I hear from Cook that he spends most of his time in the great cabin with his charts and his instruments. He's not a big man, but any time I've seen him tour the ship, he certainly commands respect. He keeps his short black beard trimmed to a point, and that gives him a stern, forbidding sort of appearance. I don't think I've ever seen him smile.

Today Captain James ordered me to report to the great cabin. When I arrived, he was seated at a large table, hunched over a leather-bound book in which he was writing hurriedly.

"Jeremy," he said, waving his arm to beckon me in, "pull up a stool and sit down."

I swallowed and replied nervously, "Yes, sir."

I perched on the edge of the stool and looked around. There was a firebox on one wall and a bench on the other that served as the Captain's bed. Otherwise, the table took up most of the space.

Captain James pushed the book aside. He looked straight at me. "Now, Jeremy, how are you getting on with your work?"

At first I found him too frightening to talk to, but he quickly put me at ease with a small smile.

"Would you like to see what I record in the logbook?"

He slid the book across the table, and I looked at the latest entry:

May 18, 1631,
Latitude: 51°26' north with Blasket's bearing northeast about 12 leagues away. Wind direction: N.W. Seas: Fair. Heading: West Northwest.
Weather: foggy, misty and wet.

While I was reading the log, he bustled about unrolling charts, arranging and rearranging his instruments and talking on and on about the mission.

"Jeremy," he said, jabbing his finger at a place on a chart, "we are going to see sights that no one in England has ever seen, and it is important that we record everything from tidal currents to ice conditions. Look here," he moved his hand over a blank space on the chart, "these are waters never sailed in. Maps must be drawn, experiments carried out and results carefully and accurately noted."

"But sir, I thought we were looking for a northwest passage. Isn't that what the mission is about?"

He held up a hand. "True, we are trying to expand trade for English merchants, but we are also trying to expand our knowledge about the northern parts of the world."

He got even more excited now and picked up several instruments he had bought himself and provided for the voyage. He talked about quadrants and staves and compasses. Compasses, now that caught my attention. All I could think of was the trouble they had caused Will on the day we reported to the ship.

The Lieutenant had brought us to the great cabin to meet Captain James. While we were waiting for him to arrive, Will had reached out and touched one of the compasses on the Captain's table. He didn't mean anything by it. He didn't even pick it up. The Lieutenant whirled around, twisted Will's arm behind his back and started shouting at him.

"Ow, you're breaking my arm," Will howled.

"Break it? I'll do better than that. I'll beat the bad manners out of your skin for a year." And he swore quite violently.

The Lieutenant is big and wide-shouldered, which makes him even more threatening. I feared he would break Will's arm. Afterwards, I was angry with myself for being too timid to speak up and plead for Will's safety. Fortunately Captain James stepped into the cabin just in time.

"Enough!" the Captain said stiffly.

"Sir, I caught him . . ."

"I said that is enough. You are dismissed."

"Sir!" snapped the Lieutenant.

He stomped out of the cabin with his bad temper oozing out of him. As he passed me, he rolled his eyes in the direction of the Captain and cursed under his breath. By the look on his face, I was going to be surprised if this was the end of the matter as far as he was concerned.

I put this thought from my mind and came back to the present. Captain James was trying to interest me in the mission, so I took the opportunity to ask him how long he thought we would be away. He linked his arms behind his back, something I notice he does when he is thinking, and paced back and forth. Then he paused, rested his eyes on me for a moment and said, "When we undertake voyages of discovery, Jeremy, there are difficulties and hazards that no one can predict. With luck we might be back within a year. If we are unlucky . . . well, let's just say we have enough provisions to stay away for two years."

I was sore flustered when I heard that. My stomach tried to force its way up through my throat. I didn't think I could survive being away two years. I thanked the Captain and staggered out of the great cabin blinded by tears. "Who am I?" I thought. "What am I doing here?" I had the strangest feeling that the Jeremy I thought I knew had been stolen by the Little People and that I was a changeling living someone else's life.

Becoming Historians

History offers us so many opportunities for dramatic exploration, but we need to make clear whether we are (a) following the exact events of the history (such as retelling the stories of flood victims), (b) exploring details that underpin the event (as in a historical fiction novel), or (c) imagining *what if* . . . and exploring and altering what happened into what might have happened if . . . Reflection after the drama can present time for clarifying, comparing, and contrasting the different accounts from history and from drama.

Modes of dramatic exploration

- *Using Issues, Themes, Characters, and Conflict:* Enactment involves dramatizing a historical incident or event from documented information; however, a simple recounting does not create drama. There must be new discovery, new learning, for drama to be happening during the enactment.

  The students read or hear the story, discuss it, and then decide how to enact it. They must understand who they will be, where and when the action takes place, and what they are going to do. They then can begin the action and improvise the dialogue. Rather than re-creating details and plot line, the students use the issues, the themes, the characters, and the conflict as a beginning for dramatic exploration. They may dramatize the problem of the action, or re-examine the incidents from a new perspective. It must not be a mere staging of the known facts — it must create a new telling, using the concepts and the details of the historical event.

- *Delving into Stories Within the History Story:* After investigating a historical time, students can elaborate upon the subtextual information. A minor detail may provide the stimulus for an improvised scene; or peripheral characters may be expanded as the students explore motivations and relationships. Questions the students raise as they probe for deeper insights into a situation can provide the stimulus for drama.
- *Considering Personal Implications:* Using a story as a basis, teachers can present the students with more problems related to it or alter the events of the story. The students can invent their own story dramas from any implications for their own lives that they see in the history.
- *Flashing Back and Forward:* This convention is used to provide different perspectives on the action in a drama. Scenes can be explored from an earlier time (flashback) to explain the causes of an action in the present. Students can also show an action in a later time by considering its imagined or actual outcome (flash-forward).

Historians in role

To become historians in the drama, the students can use headlines as moments for exploration in the life of Ludie, a character in Cynthia Rylant's novel *Ludie's Life*. The author returns to her home state of West Virginia with this evocative collection of poems that create a powerful narrative that flows like a novel. The reader follows Ludie from childhood to falling in love and getting married in a hardscrabble coal-mining town, through the birth of her own children, through happy times, heartache, and loss, into old age, still imagining her husband Rupe was beside her, until passing away at 100 years old.

Ludie's Life

It was a beautiful morning when Ludie died,
just the kind of April morning she loved.
She'd get up early and go out to the kitchen
 to make a pot of coffee,
the sun rising just over the mountains,
and dew on the grass.
It was so quiet these mornings.
Ludie would sit at the round kitchen table
Rupe had pulled from a barn years ago
and watch the birds at the feeder.
The trees all glistened silver in the light
and the world was
calm as heaven.
Was it any wonder, then, that Ludie
chose to die just before dawn?
How else would she have

See the Glossary, "Overview of Drama Conventions," for a summary of drama conventions described in this book.

caught the morning in this,
her final moment on the earth?
She would have wanted to take one last look
at the small white house in the mountains,
at the dirt road which had always led her home.
She would have wanted to say good-bye.
Somewhere Ludie was going to find
everything she had ever lost.
And she would go looking . . .
just as soon as Rupe finished his coffee,
and all the birds had flown.

— *Cynthia Rylant*

A Day in the Life: The excerpt "Ludie" ends the poetic novel *Ludie's Life* and lets the students reflect on the century of life experience this woman lived through. To help deepen their understanding of what those years held, the students can locate newspaper headlines from 1900 to 2000, and use the content to fashion a history of Ludie's life. One Internet source is Newseum (www.newseum.org), which offers headlines from all of her years. Students in partners or groups can then develop their work.

Each pair can select one day from one decade in Ludie's life. Using newspaper headlines, they can establish an event that connects her life to the headline. (What did those around her say about this event? What was her family doing that year? What did she and her husband discuss?) The class can then create a sequence of brief, improvised scenes of four or five lines built around the days in the life of Ludie, representing all 10 decades. The scenes can then be shared in a chronological order, and afterwards, students can revise their scenes from the information gleaned from seeing the entire events of her lifetime. The following headlines are samples of those events of the times in her life. They can act as a resource, or students can research others, perhaps on a single theme or issue. They will be painting with words and actions 100 years of Ludie's life.

Sat., Jan. 6, 1900 Boers attack at Ladysmith, about 1,000 killed or injured
Mon., Jan 3, 1910 British miners strike for 8 hour working day
Sat. Jan. 3 1920 NY Yankees purchase Babe Ruth from Red Sox for $125,000
Mon. Jan. 20, 1930 Clyde Tombaugh Discovers Pluto (1930)
Fri. Jan. 26, 1940 Nazis forbid Polish Jews to travel on trains
Sun. Jan. 15, 1950 4,000 attend National Emergency Civil Rights Conference in Washington DC
Sat. Jan. 2, 1960 John F Kennedy announces run for US Presidency
Mon. Jan., 12, 1970 Boeing 747 makes its maiden voyage
Fri. Jan. 18, 1980 Gold reaches $1,000 an ounce
Sun. Jan. 14, 1990 "Simpsons" premiered on Fox-TV
Mon., Jan.1, 2000 World enters new century smoothly

Guided Tour: Students can lead each other on a guided tour of Ludie's home. The information they earlier researched about the history of world events that surrounded the 100 years of Ludie's life can form the statements that students give as the tour proceeds, and could be accompanied by photographs they have found and captions that highlight the incidents. Some students may wish to bring in from home evocative objects, such as a lace handkerchief, that symbolize an incident or memory in Ludie's life. Alternatively, students can create tableaux to portray the times, with spoken headlines. As they guide someone through the space, they can provide descriptions and narration, or answer questions in order to give background and significance to the events and people in the century of Ludie's life.

Teaching Technique: Side-Coaching

The teacher gives encouraging or descriptive commentary as the students act out their ideas in the drama. By suggesting actions and ideas the students might explore, the teacher helps sustain the drama's momentum. Sometimes, only a few students need side-coaching; sometimes, the whole class requires it. The teacher must go where needed. The teacher's voice can give confidence to nervous or insecure students or inject enthusiasm into a lacklustre activity. The teacher can point out story ideas or remind the students of ideas mentioned in discussion that could be incorporated. The suggestions should be tentative, and the teacher should not try to impose ideas on the group. In general, the teacher as side-coach constantly gives oral reinforcement.

Challenging or Conflicting Positions

Drama is an effective way to support sustained discussion on a topic. It also provides students with a way to try out unpopular ideas using voices not their own. In this way, students gain the opportunity to reflect on the consequences of differing positions.

In the work described here, a teacher focused on conflicting viewpoints presented in a poem and used drama strategies to enable her students to rehearse and develop their thinking as they considered different perspectives on the bullying taking place.

In order to help her students gain the confidence of their own impressions, the teacher set up a close reading activity. She grouped the students in fours and asked one volunteer in each group to act as chair and recorder.

Before this the teacher had read the poem aloud to the class without comment. She directed the groups to read the poem on their own silently, then out loud in unison. Following this, the students went back to the poem and read it silently and slowly, paying attention to anything they noticed or that popped into their minds. When everyone had had a few minutes of quiet time with the poem, each chair asked each group member to share one thing noticed. The chairs recorded these observations on chart paper. When each group member (including the chair) had taken a turn, a second and third round followed. Some students noticed the story, some noticed mental pictures based on the senses, some noticed personal feelings evoked by the situation, and others noticed patterns of sound and specific vocabulary.

At the conclusion of this activity, each group was asked to give a one-minute report of its findings. The teacher chaired the meeting, complimenting the groups on their observations and summarizing each group's contribution to the session.

The students took away a good working knowledge of the poem and engaged confidently in the following drama activities.

Creating circular theatre

- Individual stanzas were assigned to groups, and tableaux were developed to illustrate the action in the stanzas. One member of each group read the stanza aloud.
- Working in pairs, the students created improvisations, one minute long, that revealed one thing the character Jane had observed about the physical, social, or emotional dynamics of the class. Jane, the students agreed, was aware of many of the tensions in the classroom to which others seemed oblivious.
- Students gathered in a circle to play their scenes. Unlike a carousel, where scenes are presented one after another in a specified order, the teacher employed circular theatre, which is improvisational in its execution. The teacher approached a pair of students and signaled them to play their scene. Suddenly, she turned her back on them and approached another pair as the former faded out. The teacher continued in this fashion, sampling scenes, going back to revisit scenes already played in order to connect story threads that were emerging. Sometimes, the teacher improvised with a pair in role as the teacher in the poem. Thus, the students heard snatches of conversation from a variety of viewpoints and discovered a broader range of possibilities for thinking about the main characters.

Thinking in collective role

- Students worked in pairs, taking the roles of Jane and Jimmy. Jane, upset about Jimmy's treatment of Bill in class, took the viewpoint that the cycle of bullying doesn't end with more bullying. Jimmy's viewpoint was to argue that the only way to stop a bully was to stand up to the person. The students improvised for one minute.

Note that students could be asked to speak as the character's former self, present self, or future self.

- Students who played Jimmy were invited to sit in a circle on the floor with the teacher. Students who played Jane stood behind their Jimmy. This Inner/Outer Circle strategy involved the students in collective role. All the seated students spoke as Jimmy. Those standing spoke as Jane.
- The teacher began by questioning the inner circle about what happened after class when Jane met Jimmy in the schoolyard. At first only one or two students spoke, but as the questioning continued, more joined in. The students in the outer circle listened and observed until they were addressed by the teacher.

  In questioning the students in collective role, the teacher made suggestions, analyzed what a character was saying, challenged the character to think along a different line, and made certain that the case for each side had been adequately made.
- The teacher asked the students who played Jane to write in role to Jimmy about the disagreement they had. She challenged them to think about their position, the potential harm to their friendship, and what they might say to relieve some of the tension. The students who played Jimmy wrote in role to those playing Jane.

Thinking critically out of role

- The students formed a line across the classroom. The teacher read a position statement: "The only way to stop bullying is to stand up to the bully." She asked those who strongly agreed to move to the left of the line. Those who strongly disagreed were prompted to move to the right. Those who mildly

agreed were asked to move towards the centre left. Those who mildly disagreed were asked to move towards the centre right.

- The teacher then interviewed the students on the left of the continuum. Next, she interviewed the students on the right. Finally, she went to the middle and interviewed the students there.
- She asked the students if any of them wished to change positions on the continuum now that they had listened to all the arguments. A few moments were taken up with shifting of positions.
- The teacher then asked the students to turn to a partner and explain why they had changed or not changed positions in the line.

Here is the poem that provoked such involvement.

The Bully Asleep

One afternoon, when grassy
Scents through the classroom crept,
Bill Craddock laid his head
Down on his desk, and slept.

The students came round him:
Jimmy, Roger, and Jane;
They lifted his head timidly
And let it sink again.

'Look, he's gone sound asleep, Miss,'
Said Jimmy Adair;
'He stays up all the night, you see;
His mother doesn't care.'

'Stand away from him, students.'
Miss Andrews stooped to see.
'Yes, he's asleep; go on
With your writing, and let him be.'

'Now's a good chance!' whispered Jimmy;
And he snatched Bill's pen and hid it.
'Kick him under the desk, hard;
He won't know who did it.'

'Fill all his pockets with rubbish —
Paper, apple-cores, chalk.'
So they plotted, while Jane
Sat wide-eyed at their talk.

Not caring, not hearing,
Bill Craddock he slept on;
Lips parted, eyes closed —
Their cruelty gone.

'Stick him with pins!' muttered Roger.
'Ink down his neck!' said Jim.
But Jane, tearful and foolish,
Wanted to comfort him.

— *John Walsh*

Acting on Information

In the following lesson, the whole class in role came together within the framework of a formal gathering or meeting. In such a meeting, the teacher and the students adopt roles with differing points of view and discuss a problem as if they are characters in a play. This strategy allows the teacher to introduce new information, inject tension, and create mood. The impetus for the meeting here was the poem "Alone in the Grange," by Gregory Harrison.

Visualizing "Alone in the Grange"

The class first had a pertinent discussion about rumors and how they can be harmful when they create doubt, hostility, and fear.

After requesting that the students listen with eyes closed in order to visualize everything in their mind's eye, the teacher read aloud the poem "Alone in the Grange."

At the end of the reading, the students were asked to keep their eyes closed and concentrate on the picture they found most powerful. The teacher passed among the students, touching them lightly on the shoulder and asking for a description of one detail in their mental pictures.

The students as a class prepared the poem for choral speaking. They considered lines best spoken by the whole class and lines that would make good solos. They experimented speaking the lines in different ways, for example, reading as if the text is a secret that mustn't be overheard or reading as if it is an insult.

If walls and furniture could speak — physical theatre

Side-Coach Note: Modeling

This strategy — physical theatre — may have to be modeled a few times to stimulate student thinking and build confidence.

Students were asked to think about the appearance of the outside of the old man's house. One at a time, they were given the opportunity to take up a position in open space and portray a part of the exterior of the house. Each student stated what he or she was and added one fact. For example: "I am the front window. I haven't been washed in years." The scene built cumulatively until every member of the group was in place.

The teacher approached the house, telling the students, "If the house could speak, what might it say? If I stop in front of you, make a statement." (As an example, one student portraying a door said, "Go away! My hinges are rusty. It pains me to move.")

Side-Coach Note: Poses on Hold

If students adopt strenuous poses, have them retain their spots but in neutral position until all students are in place. At this point have everyone resume his or her stance.

The teacher invited the students to explore inside the house in the same fashion, only this time they were to reveal something about the old man who lived there. Students in one half of the class entered the playing space one at a time, adopted a position as something belonging to the old man, and added one fact about him. (For example: "I am the old man's reading chair. He has rested on my arms for over 50 years.") When the first half was in place, the other half of the class asked questions of the objects in order to learn more about the old man. Then the spectator group took its turn.

At the conclusion of the drama, the students discussed who they thought was telling the story of the old man in the Grange and what clues they had about the speaker's feelings towards him.

From formal meeting to corridor of voices

In another class, the teacher took the role of the narrator and assigned the students the role of social workers. She explained to the students that they would attend a meeting in role. The reason for the meeting would be made clear once the drama started. The students were told that at this stage, their main job was to ask questions, not provide solutions.

In her opening remarks, in role, the teacher introduced herself as a neighbor of the old man who lived in the Grange and who was concerned for his safety because of repeated acts of vandalism. She explained that action needed to be taken, but she didn't know where to begin because the old man was unwilling to seek help.

The class questioned the teacher-in-role to gather as much information as they could. In groups of four they huddled together to review facts and think about solutions. When decisions had been taken, a corridor of voices was formed and the teacher-in-role walked slowly down the corridor, listening to advice. One side of the corridor offered action strategies; the other side argued that privacy must be respected. At the end, the teacher summarized her thoughts and announced a decision.

For "Alone in the Grange," the session ended with a debriefing in which students shared stories about people who lived alone and were sometimes the subject of curiosity on the part of others. The teacher asked the students how they behaved around such individuals and invited them to share their ideas and concerns. As is the case with any situation belonging to fiction, each student brought his or her life experiences and understanding to it, and the teacher was enabled to extend the thinking of the class. From the safe position of the views of fictional characters whose lives they had entered, the students could tackle tough questions.

Here is the text of the poem.

Alone in the Grange

Strange, Strange,
Is the little old man
Who lives in the Grange
Old,
Old,
And they say that he keeps
A box full of gold.
Bowed,
Bowed,
Is his thin little back
That once was so proud.

Soft,
Soft,
Are his steps as he climbs
The stairs to the loft.
Black,
Black,
Is the old shuttered house,
Does he sleep on a sack?

They say he does magic,
That he can cast spells,
That he prowls round the garden
Listening for bells;

That he watches for strangers,
Hates every soul,
And peers with his dark eye
Through the keyhole.

I wonder, I wonder,
As I lie in my bed,
Whether he sleeps with his hat
    On his head?
    Is he really a magician
    With altar of stone,
    Or a lonely old gentleman
    Left on his own?

— *Gregory Harrison*

This chapter has explored how we construct drama through the integration of factual information with imaginative creations. All stories of history do this every time a conversation is written, because, of course, no one was present to record exactly what was said. By locating information about a particular time or the people who lived then, or by revisiting an event or a place, students can be the authoritative voices: those with the knowledge. They can try on the Mantle of the Expert, and the drama can develop around them. Students can also add details of information to their improvisations, bits and pieces from lived experiences or from books or films, even invented things that add to the texture of their work, shadows that deepen the imagination, data that add reality to their inventions. The information may not be altogether accurate, but the intent of the drama makers is to add that sense of "real" to the imaginary worlds of drama.

10

Reading Words Aloud

Reading aloud can be connected to drama in four ways: (1) sharing rehearsed selections — poems, songs, and scripts that may lead to dramatic exploration; (2) presenting selections in Readers Theatre that have previously been the basis for the dramatic exploration; (3) reading aloud in role pieces within the drama, such as letters, proclamations, points of debate, songs, and chants; and (4) reflecting orally about the drama from personal journals, poems, and related materials students have generated that may illuminate the work. Most students need assistance in working in an oral reading situation, and drama strategies provide support in this area.

Scripts for young people are now available for use in schools, and novel excerpts, poems, and picture books can be excellent sources of good dialogue that may easily be adapted for oral reading activities. Students can work in pairs or in small groups, reading the dialogue silently and then aloud. Teachers can alter the experience in several ways. For example, they can have the students change roles, they can introduce new settings or tensions, and they can change the time period. The goal is to help students interpret the selection in such a way that they can discover new meaning in it.

Readers Theatre is a technique for reading aloud stories and poems as if they were scripts. The actual words are used, and the narration, along with the dialogue, offers a set of exciting problems for students to explore. The selections used for Readers Theatre can then be used within the drama work as a stimulus or source of tension that adds to the playmaking.

Readers Theatre can contribute to both ends of a drama work too. The exercise of creating a Readers Theatre demonstration can serve as the beginning of the drama work, as the students build on events to create a frame for dramatic exploration. In "Creating Parallel Stories," in Chapter 8, poems from the novel *Ann and Seamus* are included as texts to be explored for reading aloud, to set the scene, and to give a particular context to the drama that will follow. As well, the shared oral reading of a text can close a unit of drama, as suggested in the *Ann and Seamus* unit.

The point to remember in working with text read aloud, as in Readers Theatre, is that the meanings within the words, the ideas and feelings within the lines, need to be explored in order to be revealed. This necessity forms the basis for truly interpreting a selection so that the activity does not become rote, unrehearsed parroting of the words. Drama strategies can be a means of allowing students to examine the themes within the printed text they have been given, and improvisation based on a text becomes a tool for the exploration of the original text's ideas, relationships, and language. It is important that much of the drama be not just the oral reading of a text, but a living through of its concepts.

Students can read aloud poems, songs, excerpts from novels and stories, or their own compositions, and can explore various interpretations of them. Working in small groups, students can select the interpretation they wish to give the words. They can even devise ways to express the text in dramatic terms, establishing spatial relationships among the characters and making specific recommendations (about tone, volume, and pace) on how to speak the words.

Inside the drama structure, participants can read aloud documents, parables, lectures, and excerpts found through research where the role play gives added strength to the belief in and commitment to the work. These resources can be created previously to the drama work by the teacher or the students, or within the drama as a response to an event. Perhaps students in role as soldiers create a letter composed by their commander explaining why the fighting must continue, feeding new strength and tension to the dramatic unit. Perhaps documents, such as an edict written by an unfair ruler to his subjects, incorporating formal language patterns and vocabulary and read aloud, can provide a powerful stimulus for continuing the role play. Similarly, a will read by the teacher as a lawyer, a deed outlining land borders, or a map showing an unknown trail, generated before or during the unit, can build belief in the action of the drama.

Joining the Choir

For many students, being a part of the whole class as they explore a choral selection offers opportunities to participate without the pressure to speak alone, as in singing in a choir. These collective ensembles offer a level of comfort that can strengthen the efforts of some students and move them forward into other independent activities. On the other hand, some students relish the opportunity to take a specific part, and this can offer variation in who reads the lines — individuals, soloists, small groups, a chorus, the class in two sections, as in a play script.

We like the students to help in the decision making. They can give input into who will read which lines, how the lines could be said, and what is the desired mood. Students can offer ideas on the pace at which the words should be spoken, the volume (from shouts to whispers), the emphasis on certain words or lines, the need for a pause to add tension or create effect, rhythm, and perhaps the use of sound effects.

If students have their own copies, you can have them mark the copies with cues to indicate stress or pauses, or to signify the speakers of the lines. Otherwise, you might show the words on a SMART Board.

A. Experimenting with lines

The following poem by Robert Louis Stevenson is a good vehicle for letting every student join in, tasting the words and breathing life into the text. After reading silently and then listening to the teacher read the poem, students can begin to offer suggestions for interpreting the words, exploring different ways of reading the lines and the use of pauses to add power, reading on past the end of a line onto the next line rather than stopping at the line break.

Windy Nights

Whenever the moon and stars are set,
　Whenever the wind is high,
All night long in the dark and wet,
　A man goes riding by.
Late in the night when the fires are out,

Why does he gallop and gallop about?
Whenever the trees are crying aloud,
   And ships are tossed at sea,
By, on the highway, low and loud,
   By at the gallop goes he.
By at the gallop he goes, and then
By he comes back at the gallop again.

— *Robert Louis Stevenson*

The class can begin by just reading the words aloud in unison from a copy or on a SMART Board. Then, invite them to decide where to pause, which lines to speak quietly or loudly, and what the rhythm should be. ("Shall we all imitate the gallop of the horse and rider?) They can explore different paces for the reading, and try out group and solo parts.

As the work progresses, volunteers can take solo lines, groups can alternate lines, and so on. The final reading should satisfy the class, and then the poem can be reread at times throughout the year for guests.

B. Creating a mood together

The poem "The Rescue" by Ian Serraillier is an excellent resource for exploring the ways in which a text can be read together. If the students have copies, they can decide where the voice breaks should come: Where will they pause? take a breath? speed up? slow down? raise their voices? whisper? How will they handle the rhythmic pace of the poem so that a mood is created? Will they read the lines independently, or read some in unison or in groups? How will they build to a climax so that the story holds attention? Students can mark their copies, perhaps placing a vertical line to indicate a stop or a wavy underline to show whispers. A SMART Board can also hold the words, and cue marks can be inserted by students.

The Rescue

The wind is loud,
The wind is blowing,
The waves are big,
The waves are growing.
What's that? What's that?
A dog is crying,
It's in the sea,
A dog is crying.
His or hers
Or yours or mine?
A dog is crying,
A dog is crying.

Is no one there?
A boat is going,
The waves are big,
A man is rowing,
The waves are big,
The waves are growing.

Where's the dog?
It isn't crying.
His or hers
Or yours or mine?
Is it dying?
Is it dying?

The wind is loud,
The wind is blowing,
The waves are big,
The waves are growing.
Where's the boat?
It's upside down.
And where's the dog,
And must it drown?
His or hers
Or yours or mine?
O, must it drown?
O, must it drown?

Where's the man?
He's on the sand,
So tired and wet
He cannot stand.
And where's the dog?
It's in his hand,
He lays it down
Upon the sand.
His or hers
Or yours or mine?
The dog is mine,
The dog is mine!

So tired and wet
And still it lies.
I stroke its head,
It opens its eyes,
It wags its tail,
So tired and wet.
I call its name,
For it's my pet,
Not his or hers
Or yours, but mine—
And up it gets,
And up it gets!

— *Ian Serraillier*

C. Interpreting lines and what's between them

In reading a narrative selection or a poem, some students can act as narrators while others read the bits of dialogue. When students begin to omit such lines as "he said" or "replied John," they are beginning to interpret the words, touching upon the sense of theatre that such an activity develops. There are dozens of options, however. For example, a character who speaks dialogue may also read the information or thoughts found in the narrative that refer to his or her role. Several characters can read narration as a chorus or repeat lines as an echo or refrain. We are amazed by the ingenuity of students when faced with making "out-loud" sense of a narrative selection — they see it as a puzzle, to be tried and treated until the whole picture is evident.

"Switch on the Night" appears on page 108.

The poem "Switch on the Night" by Ray Bradbury uses narration as its main structure, with two characters having dialogue. This format offers students opportunities for interpreting narration orally: Who will say the different lines? Who will the speakers be in role? Why are they saying these lines with the boy and girl present? Who is Night? Why has she appeared? Why does the boy need courage? As the students explore such questions, they are beginning to interpret the lines, building a context for their own shared reading.

You can help students select their lines and mark where they feel they should pause, where they should breathe, how quickly they should speak, when they should whisper, and so on. There are many questions for them to consider, these among them: When will everyone say lines together? When should the narration be read by one student? Should students join in at times, building a cumulative sound? What visuals should be seen as the poem is spoken? Where should readers sit or stand? Should there be movement with the lines? What should everyone wear?

The questions will grow if the class decides to build a drama event around the poem after interpreting it aloud. Students may ask themselves: What shall we begin with? Who or what could the girl called Night represent? Who could we be in this playmaking session, so that there are many roles? Who were the children playing on the night lawns? Shall we use the lines or improvise as well? Does the darkness return? What could it mean? Shall we explore these ideas in groups, and bring back the shared ideas in order to create an ensemble play with everyone involved? (See "Building an Ensemble Drama," page 133.) Do we need musical instruments or taped music? Can we find a dark space in the school to create mood and atmosphere so that we can share both the poem and the drama experience?

In one Grade 5 classroom, the class decided that the girl had been sent by her planet to tell those on Earth to turn their artificial lights off to control the enemies called "The Darkness." The class moved to a stairwell, and the girl, standing on the landing and accompanied by two "spirits" who could offer her advice, held the beam of a flashlight to her face, as she answered the questions of the people below. The drama work, through the questions and answers, evolved into a narrative of "The Darkness" searching for another planet full of continual light to take over, and by persuading everyone to keep their world "shining in darkness" for 48 hours, the enemy would bypass them.

Readers Theatre: From Print Text to Voice Text

With some physical arrangement, such as stools for the speakers or a pool of light within which the group can work, Readers Theatre provides a perfect opportunity for oral interpretation, as well as a vehicle for dramatic exploration.

Readers Theatre scripts abound, but it is good practice for students to use their own creativity in adapting a selection for performance. Let students know that a character who speaks dialogue may also read the information or thoughts found

Switch on the Night

Once there was a little boy
who didn't like the Night.

He liked
Lanterns and lamps
and
torches and tapers
and
beacons and bonfires
and flashlights and flares.
But he didn't like the Night.

He didn't like light switches at all
Because light switches turned off
the yellow lamps
the green lamps
the white laps
the hall lights
the house lights
the lights in all the room.
He wouldn't touch a light switch.

And he wouldn't go out to play
after dark.
He was very lonely.
And unhappy.
For he saw, from his window,
the other children playing on the
    summer-night lawns.
In and out of the dark and
lamplight ran by children . . .
happily.

But where was our little boy?
Up in his room.
With lanterns and lamps
and flashlights
and candles and chandeliers.
All by himself.
He liked only the sun.
The yellow sun.
He didn't like
the Night.

When it was time for Mother and
    Father
to walk around switching off all the
lights . . .
One by one.

One by one.
The porch lights
the parlor lights
the pale lights
the pink lights
the pantry lights
The stairs lights . . .
Then the little boy hid in his bed.

Late at night
His was the only room
with a light
in all the town.

And then one night
With his father away on a trip
And his mother gone to bed early,
The little boy wandered alone,
All alone through the house.

My, how he had the lights blazing!
the parlor lights
the porch lights
the pantry lights
the pale lights
the pink lights
the hall lights
the kitchen lights
even the *attic* lights!
The house looked like it was on fire!
But still the little boy was alone.
While the other children played
on the night lawns
Laughing.
Far away.

All of a sudden he hard
a rap at the window!
Something dark was there.
A knock on the screen door.
Something dark was there!
A tap at the back porch.
Something dark was there!

All of a sudden someone said 'Hello!'
And a little girl stood there in the
    middle of
the white lights, the bright lights,
the hall lights, the small lights,
the yellow lights, the mellow lights.

'My name is Dark,' she said.
And she had dark hair,
and dark eyes,
and wore a dark dress
and dark shoes.
But her face was as white as the
    moon.
And the lights in her eyes
shone like white stars.

'You're lonely,' she said.

'Think what you're missing!
Have you ever thought of
switching on the crickets,
switching on the frogs,

switching on the stars,
and the great big white moon?'

'No,' said the little boy.

'Well, lets try it,' said Dark.
And they did.

They climbed up and down stairs,
switching on the Night.
Switching on the dark.
Letting the Night live in every room.
Like a frog.
Or a cricket.
Or a star.
Or a moon.

And they switched on the crickets.
And they switched on the frogs.
And they switched on the white, ice-
    cream moon.

'Oh, I like this!' said the little boy.
'Can I switch on the Night always?'

'Of course!' said Dark, the little girl.
And then she vanished.

And now the little boy is very happy.
He likes the Night.
Now he has a Night-switch instead of
    a light-switch!

He likes switches now.
He threw away his candles
and flashlights
and lamplights.
And any night in summer that you
    wish
you can see him
switching on the white moon,
switching on the red stars,
switching on the blue stars,
the green stars, the light stars,
the white stars,
switching on the frogs, the crickets,
    and Night.

And running in the dark, on the
    lawns,
with the happy children . . .
Laughing.

— *Ray Bradbury*

in the narrative that refer to his or her role. Some readers can handle dialogue; some can act as narrators. Several characters might read the narration as a chorus or repeat lines as an echo or refrain. Sound effects, such as a spring drum, a rainstick, or an alarm clock to signify morning, could be used to enhance the dialogue, or the students could snap their fingers to accentuate the rhythmic chorus. Challenge students to find ways to turn narration into direct speech and to condense long narrative descriptions. Readers Theatre is an interpretive art form, sometimes taking a form different from the original text: as in turning a novel into a film, we work with the interpretation the mode demands.

Students can experiment with staging. Will they sit on stools, backs to the audience, turning around when it's their turn to read? Will they stand behind a line of music stands in a pool of light? Will they arrange chairs horizontally and sit sideways one behind the other, turning in and out as reading turns occur, as in a poem filled with dialogue? With such potential, the activity provides a perfect opportunity for dramatic exploration as well as oral interpretation.

When students undertake such activity, initially the work often benefits from the use of short selections. These could include folk tales, Aesop's fables, urban legends, and narrative poems. Whatever the source, try to find selections that poet Kevin Crossley-Holland describes as "word bright." "How Jack Went to Seek His Fortune," included here, possesses just such a quality.

Becoming familiar with the print text

Whether students are working with a narrative poem such as "The Rescue" (pages 105–6) or a story, they should read the piece out loud several times. They might read in unison, or they could do an ensemble reading in which group members sit facing one another and the lines are read by the first reader up to the next punctuation mark. When that is reached, the next group member reads and so it continues. With a poem like "The Rescue," individual readers will have very short lines. After the first go round, the readers could read until they reach those punctuation marks indicating a full stop.

After at least three readings, the group can discuss any words, expressions, or actions they don't understand.

Casting parts comes next. Encourage the students to experiment with different possibilities for the voices and to trade parts frequently before setting the final casting. Have them include animal sounds wherever possible. When groups have rehearsed, pair them off to perform for each other.

How Jack Went to Seek His Fortune

Once upon a time there was a boy named Jack,
and one morning he started to go and seek his
fortune.
He hadn't gone very far before he met a cat.
"Where are you going, Jack?" said the cat.
"I am going to seek my fortune."
"May I go with you?"
"Yes," said Jack, "the more the merrier."

So on they went, jiggelty-jolt, jiggelty-jolt.
They went a little further and they met a dog.
"Where are you going, Jack?" said the dog.
"I am going to seek my fortune."

"May I go with you?"
"Yes," said Jack, "the more the merrier."
So on they went, jiggelty-jolt, jiggelty-jolt.
They went a little further and they met a goat.
"Where are you going, Jack?" said the goat.
"I am going to seek my fortune."
"May I go with you?"
"Yes," said Jack, "the more the merrier."
So on they went, jiggelty-jolt, jiggelty-jolt.
They went a little further and they met a bull.
"Where are you going, Jack?" said the bull.
"I am going to seek my fortune."
"May I go with you?"
"Yes," said Jack, "the more the merrier."
So on they went, jiggelty-jolt, jiggelty-jolt.
They went a little further and they met a rooster.
"Where are you going, Jack?"
"May I go with you?"
"Yes," said Jack, "the more the merrier."
So on they went, jiggelty-jolt, jiggelty-jolt.

Well, they went on till it was about dark, and they began
To think of someplace where they could spend the night.
About this time they came in sight of a house, and Jack
told them to keep still while he went up and looked in
through the window. And there were some robbers
counting over their money. Then Jack went back and
told them to wait till he gave the word, and then to make
all the noise they could. So when they were all ready
Jack gave the word, and the cat mewed, and the dog
barked, and the goat bleated, and the bull bellowed, and
the rooster crowed, and all together they made such a
dreadful noise that it frightened the robbers all away.
And then they went in and took possession of the
house. Jack was afraid the robbers would come back in
the night, and so when it came time to go to bed he
put the cat in the rocking-chair, and he put the dog under
the table, and he put the goat upstairs, and he put the
bull in the cellar, and the rooster flew up on to the roof,
and Jack went to bed.

By-and-by the robbers saw it was all dark and they
sent one man back to the house to look after their money.
Before long he came back in a great fright and told them
his story.

"I went back to the house," said he, "and went in and
tried to sit down in the rocking-chair, and there was an
old woman knitting, and she stuck her knitting-needles
into me." That was the cat, you know.
"I went to the table to look after the money and there
was a shoemaker under the table, and he stuck his awl

into me." That was the dog, you know.
"I started to go upstairs, and there was a man up
there threshing, and he knocked me down with his flail."
That was the goat, you know.
"I started to go down cellar, and there was a man down
there chopping wood, and he knocked me up with his
axe." That was the bull, you know.
"But I shouldn't have minded all that if it hadn't been
for that little fellow on top of the house, who kept
a-hollering, 'Chuck him up to me-e! Chuck him up
to me-e!'" Of course that was the cock-a-doodle-do.

Choral Dramatization

Given the right words, cheerleaders can whip sport fans into a frenzy of cheers and roars. Cheerleading, the chanting of work songs, responsive reading in religious services, and the singing games of children are not new to our culture. The early Greeks used a speaking chorus in their plays to provide a literary background for the drama or to relate the events of a scene. For centuries, laborers have chanted in rhythm to ease the burden of their work, worshippers have joined their religious leaders in choruses of praise and supplication, and young people have danced to the rhythm of their songs. Today, many playwrights are using choruses for special effects. Choral dramatization is an aspect of drama that involves everyone — it is truly a participation activity.

Dramatic effects in choral presentations are unlimited. Costumes, backdrops, lighting effects, projections, musical and sound accompaniment, and creative dance can help provide an acceptable and entertaining "happening." Students can be grouped in effective ways; stools, removable platforms, step ladders, or stairs may be used to achieve a variety of interesting levels.

Poetry and rhythmic prose that express universal thoughts and emotions are especially appropriate for choral speaking. Narrative and dramatic selections, with vivid word-pictures, potential action, marked rhythm, effective sound patterns, and universal ideas and emotions, are suitable for choral interpretation. Consider using poems by Edward Lear, such as "The Jumblies," Jack Prelutsky's "The Underwater Wibbles," or for middle years, ballads, both classic and modern.

There are a variety of ways that a class can engage in choral dramatization:

- The entire class can speak as a unit.
- Some selections may be divided into questions and answers, or appeals and responses; for these, the choir is divided into two alternating groups.
- Some poems may be divided into sections for solo speakers and several groups.
- If the ideas in a selection build to a climax, the number of voices may also increase, starting with a soloist, for example, and adding one group at a time until all of the voices say the climactic lines in unison.

A well-rehearsed chorus may not require a conductor for a performance. A leader within the group, positioned to be seen by all members, may be able to direct the group.

The poem "For a Girl Becoming" is written by Joy Harjo, an award-winning indigenous poet from New Mexico. Her advice for the women of her tribe provides an excellent source for choral dramatization, since the lines can be read by different voices, and there are opportunities for drama work as they are spoken. It is important that the poem retain the original intent of the poet and that we not misappropriate the culture being represented.

There are many ways to explore this excerpt from the poem and its themes: the village can be giving a send-off to a young woman leaving for university; the family can be gathered at the wedding of the young woman and her fiancé; the spirits of her parents can visit with sage advice that they wish they could have presented to her in person; archeologists have found these words at a dig in New Mexico and are reading them aloud to the volunteers, and so on.

The students have many decisions to make, as well. How will they add the physical elements of the work? Will they develop a pre-scene to begin the poem? Will they decide how the poem should be staged, who should speak, and what actions should be shown? Will they want to use visuals from slides on screen to accompany the reading? As they explore the various techniques that can build the drama, the words will take on deeper meanings, and the interpretation will be owned by the students.

For a Girl Becoming

Don't forget how you started your journey from that rainbow house,
How you traveled and will travel through the mountains and valleys
of human tests.
There are treacherous places along the way, but you can come to us.
There are lakes of tears shimmering sadly there, but you can come to us.
And valleys without horses or kindness, but you can come to us.
And angry, jealous gods and wayward humans who will hurt you, but you
    can come to us.
You will fall, but you will get back up again, because you are one of us.

And as you travel with us remember this:
Give a drink of water to all who ask, whether they be plant, creature,
human or helpful spirit;
May you always have clean, fresh, water.

Feed your neighbors. Give kind words and assistance
to all you meet long the way. We are all related in this place.
May you be surrounded with the helpfulness of family and good friends.

Grieve with the grieving, share joy with the joyful.
May you build a strong path with beautiful and truthful language.

Clean your room.
May you always have a home: a refuge from storm, a gathering place
for safety, for comfort.

Bury what needs to be buried.
Laugh easily at yourself.
May you always travel lightly and well.
Praise and give thanks for each small and large thing.
May you grow in knowledge, in compassion, in beauty.

Always within you is that day your spirit came to us
When rains come in from the Pacific to bless
They peered over mountains in response to the singing of medicine plants
Who danced back and forth in shawls of mist
Your mother labored there, so young in earthly years.

And we who love you gather here,
Pollen blows through this desert house to bless
And horses run the land, hundreds of them for you,
And you are here to bless.

— *Joy Harjo*

Monologues — Old Stories, New Meanings

It can be an exciting adventure for students to create versions of a story they think they know. Suddenly, their preconceptions are jolted, and they move into an altered state, caught in a web of changing perceptions, noticing every minute difference. The story brain is engaged.

When students experience two or more stories that are related in some way, their understanding of each is altered and enriched by the other as they make connections between their expanding lives and the stories. Often, one story prepares the reader for another one, facilitating the understanding of the subsequent story. And, of course, each new story sheds light on past story experiences, creating a changing view of the stories in the child's story repertoire.

Familiar tales allow people to play around with the ideas, characters, and action associated with them. For example, the composer Stephen Sondheim retold and reworked fairy tales in his musical *Into the Woods*. The following poem twists and turns the tales as well, and opens up the possibilities that role-playing can offer students in recasting and rethinking familiar stories. The students could decide who is giving this monologue about the problems with all these fairy-tale characters: perhaps another character from a fairy tale, a reporter who covered all of the events listed, a psychologist who is against all fairy tales being read to children, or an angry, unknown figure omitted from the tales.

Happy Endings

Red Riding Hood and her grandmother
made the wolf
into a big fur coat
and Gretel
shoved Hansel into the oven
and ate him with the witch
and the Beauty enjoyed
her long sleep
quite as much
as the awakening kiss
and the Prince might take
Cinderella to the palace
but she would insist
on scrubbing floors

and scouring pots
and getting her good clothes
covered with ashes
after all
it was what
she was used to.

— *Gail White*

A monologue is a speech given by one person or character. Before they discover what any monologue means, readers will need to read the lines many times. As they work around, under, and between the words, they will find a context and a base on which to build their interpretation. They can use improvisation as an excellent means of achieving deeper understanding.

A. Not the usual perception

The students can work with the following monologue, "One of the Seven Has Somewhat to Say." First, have them read it silently and then read it aloud several times alone. Let them know that if there are words or passages they are unclear about, they can consult with a classmate or the teacher. The prompts given below the monologue can be used to help students enter the original tale from a different perspective.

Ask the students to decide on some specific physical actions associated with their character's situation (e.g., gesturing up towards the ceiling when the dwarf says Snow White even dusts that). Encourage them to improvise the words of the speech as much as possible. Let them share the monologues they create in small groups.

One of the Seven Has Somewhat to Say

Remember how it was before she came — ?
The picks and shovels dropped beside the door,
The sink piled high, the meals any old time,
Our jackets where we'd flung them on the floor?
The mud tracked in, the clutter on the shelves.
None of us shaved, or more than halfway clean . . .
Just seven old bachelors, living by ourselves?
Those were the days, if you know what I mean.

She scrubs, she sweeps, she even dusts the ceilings:
She's made us build a tool shed for our stuff.
Dinner's at eight, the table setting's formal
And if I weren't afraid I'd hurt her feelings
I'd move, until we get her married off,
And things can gradually slip back to normal.

Ideas for exploration:
This poem offers opportunities for further role-playing situations. You can present a prompt as a stimulus for improvisation to students working individually, as a class, with partners, or in small groups.

- Could the students be complaining to each other as dwarves about the visitor who changed their home?

- Could Snow White counter the complaints at a household meeting with the dwarves?
- Could a dwarf be co-operating with the authorities to expose Snow White's hiding place? Students in a circle could observe the rendezvous with the spy and the castle agents.
- Could the class divided into two groups as dwarves be engaged in a debate about Snow White's contributions to their home life?

B. Shifting roles

With a partner, students can use "Interview," the monologue that follows, as the basis for an improvised drama. This activity will mix the lines of the monologue with the improvised dialogue.

1. Student A can begin as the stepmother giving the monologue, and student B can continue improvising dialogue as the interviewer, based on the stepmother's lines, asking questions of student A. (See sample questions below.)
2. Prompt the pairs to do the scene again, but direct each student A to respond only with physical activity — mime, gesture, movement.

Interview

Yes, this is where she lived before she won
The title Miss Glass Slipper of the Year,
And went to the ball and married the king's son.
You're from the local press, and want to hear
About her early life? Young man, sit down.
These are my *own* two daughters; you'll not find
Nicer, more biddable girls in all the town,
And lucky, I tell them, not to be the kind

That Cinderella was, spreading those lies,
Telling those shameless tales about the way
We treated her. Oh, nobody denies
That she was pretty, if you like those curls.
But looks aren't everything, I always say.
Be sweet and natural, I tell my girls,
And Mr. Right will come along, some day.

Questions for the stepmother:

- When did you first meet Cinderella?
- How did you meet your husband?
- Just what lies was Cinderella spreading?
- You seem angry. What is causing this emotional response?

C. Alter ego

Using the poem "Juvenile Court," below, students in pairs can explore character and alter ego.

Student A reads the monologue to student B, who becomes a mirror physically and repeats the words of student A line by line.

Each pair then establishes who student A represents. Student A could start off as a reporter, a relative, a neighbor, the lawyer, the judge, or a victim.

Have pairs repeat the monologue reading, but this time, student B, as the alter ego of student A, tries to express student A's real thoughts.

Tell all student A's that they are free to argue with their partners (in role) if they feel that their thoughts have not been portrayed accurately.

Student B can then give the "Juvenile Court" monologue, and student A can act as the alter ego.

Juvenile Court

Deep in the oven, where the two had shoved her,
They found the Witch, burned to a crisp, of course.
And when the police had decently removed her,
They questioned the children, who showed no remorse.
"She threatened us," said Hansel, "with a kettle
Of boiling water, just because I threw
The cat into the well," cried little Gretel.
"She fussed because I broke her broom in two,

And said she'd lock up Hansel in a cage
For drawing funny pictures on her fence."
Wherefore the court, considering their age,
And ruling that there seemed some evidence
The pair had acted under provocation,
Released them to their parents, on probation.

D. Cohesive group

Using the poem "The Marriage," one student within a group can present the monologue, and the other members can respond in role. They might interview the speaker, act as family or friends, take part in a group gathering, or be strangers meeting at a crossroads and gossiping.

The Marriage

The King and I are more than satisfied;
It's turned out better than we ever hoped.
He's good to her, she made a lovely bride.
And think how we'd have felt, if they'd eloped!
We're quite aware of what his motives were:
He wanted money, and an easy life,
But in the end we had to humor her,
And all she wanted was to be his wife.

As for that fairy tale she likes to tell
About the Frog who scrambled from the well
And gave her back her ball, all dripping wet,
Then turned into a Prince (that's how they met),
We know he's not a Prince — the point is this:
Our poor romantic daughter thinks he is.

Coming together

Students form new groups of four or five. In their groups, students discuss a frame that will hold all of the monologues A to D. One Grade 7 class decided that the characters giving the monologues were at a fairy-tale convention, and each participant chose one of the poems to read aloud in role. The students moved about the room, each speaking lines at the same time, until they found someone with the same monologue. They then began saying their poem in unison.

Each student will have to fit one of the monologues into the dramatic action. The goal of this work is to use improvised dialogue until the players can legitimately include their monologues in the small-group work. Once a group has found a way of including all of the monologues, members can present their polished scenes to the class.

The class can role-play within each monologue presented. Questions to consider:

- How will the speaker work everyone in?
- What frame will emerge to structure the work?
- Will the group be able to maintain the idea of the original poems?
- Is the character of the speaker developed by what is happening in the improvisation?

Dialogue: The Frame for Drama

Drama is built on dialogue, improvised or scripted, or combinations of both, with movement and gestures that accompany the words. Participating in a scripted dialogue allows the students to read for interpretation and to notice cues for both speaking and responding appropriately. The following poem, written for two voices, can act as a minimal script, where the context for the action is determined by the students.

1. The dialogue poem can be handled in partners, by dividing the class into two sections for choral work, or by having each line read (said) by a series of students.

What Is Moving in the Long Grasses?

Look!
  Where?
There.
  Where?
In the long grasses.
  In the long grasses?
Yes. There. Do you see it?
  What? What do I see?
It's moving. In the long grasses.
  What is? What is?
A tiger.
  A tiger?
A huge tiger.
  I can't see it. I can't see it.
It's there.
  Where?
Shhhhhh! Whisper.
In the long grasses.
  Tell me where to look.

Do you see a flash of orange?
    A flash of orange?
In the long grasses.
    I see it. I see it.
That is the tiger.
    It is moving.
Through the long grasses.
    How big is it?
Big. It is a big tiger.
    Look!
It hears. It hears us.
    Whisper. Always whisper.
It's moving again.
    The grasses move as it moves.
We see it, but we don't really see it.
    We see the grasses moving.
It is still there. Watching. Listening.
    Does it see us?
Tigers see everything.
    The tiger sees us.
It's moving again.
    It is moving through the grasses.
The tiger passes.
    The tiger passes.

— *David Booth*

2. The students can explore different contexts for the reading, and for the conversation in the poem to be heard.

For example, one class chose a jungle setting; another developed a zoo script with the characters trapped there after closing hours; and a third adopted the scenario of watching for poachers and role-played the interviews between officials and those accused of poaching wild animals.

Dramatic encounter

An unusual choice was made by a senior class. The students decided that the speakers were refugees and the tigers were the occupying soldiers. The class read the lines in two large groups, the one as the leaders of the escape and the other as the followers. The ensuing drama concerned the prisoners persuading the soldiers to let them escape, since they were originally from the same country. After the players read the lines in these new roles, in pairs, they wrote the conversation the escapees might have had with the soldiers. Two students, Damien and Kim, created the following dialogue, which could then be read by other students.

Don't move!
Stand up!
    Don't shoot!
Why not?
You are traitors.
    We are citizens.

We want to be free.
How can you call yourselves citizens
if you are sneaking out of our country?
    It is our country too.
But you are running away,
are you not?
    No! we are leaving for safety.
    Our lives are at risk.
    My family is at risk.
    We will return when the revolution is over.
At risk from who?
    From you.
We are soldiers protecting our country!
    Then let us go.
If we do, you will fight with our enemies
against our country.
    We do not fight.
    That is why we are leaving.
You are cowards!
    No! We are citizens fleeing with our children!
We cannot let you leave.
    You are from our village.
    We know your families.
    Respect us. Respect your families!
Are you armed?
    We have no weapons.
Then move. We have not seen you.
The grasses are tall. You will be invisible in them.
    We will return.
    We will return.

Exploring dialogue in other genres

- *Sifting Text for Dialogue:* Novels with much dialogue also offer texts for exploration. Students can select a passage from a novel they have read, and with a partner build a dramatic reading.
- *Improvising and Transcribing Talk:* Using an incident reported in the newspaper, groups can improvise the dialogue that might have occurred. They can then create a script through their group improvisation by acting out the incident again and recording it. With everyone sharing the task, the scene can be replayed and the dialogue transcribed. To test its effectiveness, one group can give its script to another group to perform.

Scripts and the Language of Shakespeare

Detailed study of Shakespeare's plays is not required in most elementary schools, but this is a time when younger students can be given the opportunity to become familiar with Shakespeare's words and to enjoy getting the language on the tongue as they interpret dramatic scenes through reading aloud, tableaux, improvisation, and other forms of enactment.

Macbeth is a good choice for elementary students because it is fast, exciting, and full of shadowy spirits, ghosts, characters with supernatural powers, murder, alarm bells, and treason. The play also raises many areas of discussion for students, including ambition and lust for power, friends and loyalty, conscience and guilt, and the difficulties humans experience in day-to-day life.

First, students must become familiar with the story. The teacher can read aloud from a prose source, perhaps Leon Garfield's *Shakespeare Stories*. The teacher can either narrate the story as students mime the actions spontaneously, or the play could be summarized by the teacher in the form of a chart. A BBC Animated Tales version could be viewed on YouTube. Regardless of the approach taken, it is important to introduce the students to Shakespeare's language as quickly as possible and to involve them in speaking the words.

There is no better place to start than with the opening scene, which is short, sharp, and mysterious.

Thunder and lightning. Enter three witches.

FIRST WITCH:	When shall we three meet again? In thunder, lightning, or in rain?
SECOND WITCH:	When the hurly-burly's done, When the battle's lost and won.
THIRD WITCH:	That will be ere the set of sun.
FIRST WITCH:	Where the place?
SECOND WITCH:	Upon the heath.
THIRD WITCH:	There to meet with Macbeth.
FIRST WITCH:	I come, Graymalkin.
SECOND WITCH:	Paddock calls.
THIRD WITCH:	Anon.
ALL:	Fair is foul, and foul is fair, Hover through the fog and filthy air.

Experimenting with a scene

One teacher formed her class into groups of three and had the students cast the parts and read the scene out loud. At the end of the reading, they were asked to switch parts and read the scene out loud again. This activity was repeated with new challenges issued for each reading. For example, students read the lines angrily, calmly, as if sharing a secret, as if telling a funny joke, as if standing on mountaintops far from one another, and in different emotional states — the first witch bossy, the second haughty, the third nervous and twitchy.

The teacher asked the students to speculate about the scene: Why were the characters having this conversation? What were their objectives? What was the scene's overall mood?

The teacher had the students cast the parts in their groups for the last time and challenged the students to convey a specific mood for their scene. Each student was to highlight the mood by giving his/her lines a certain voice (e.g., mysterious), emotion (e.g., excited), and action (e.g., scratching the nose). Students were also directed to plan their entrance and exit, and to add sound effects if desired.

When the groups had rehearsed their scenes, the teacher gathered the students into a carousel, put on some mysterious background music, and had the students play the scenes one after another without stopping.

When students know who the play's main characters are and have an overall sense of the plot, they can do an exploration of some or all of these key scenes:

Act I, Scene III   Macbeth and Banquo meet the witches.

Act I, Scene V   Lady Macbeth reads Macbeth's letter and determines that King Duncan must be killed. Macbeth returns to the castle.

Act II, Scene II   The murder scene: Lady Macbeth tries to calm Macbeth's fears about what he has done.

Act III, Scene IV   After the murder of Banquo, Macbeth and his wife hold a banquet which is interrupted by the appearance of Banquo's ghost.

Act IV, Scene I   Macbeth consults the witches again. They call up apparitions, one of which says he is safe until Birnam Wood comes to Dunsinane.

Act V, Scene I   Lady Macbeth walks in her sleep, haunted by guilt.

Act V, Scene V   Birnam Wood begins to move. Macbeth and his army defend Dunsinane Castle from the army led by Duncan's son. Lady Macbeth's death is reported

Trimming a scene to essentials

Scenes may require editing depending on the abilities and interests of the students. For example, when Macbeth and Banquo meet the witches for the first time (Act I, Scene III), the teacher could cut the scene as follows while still conveying the essential information:

Thunder. Enter the three witches

FIRST WITCH: Where hast thou been, sister?

SECOND WITCH: Killing swine . . .

Drum within

THIRD WITCH: A drum, a drum!
                          Macbeth doth come.

ALL: The weird sisters, hand in hand
                          Posters of the sea and land . . .
                          Thus do go about, about,
                          Thrice to thine, and thrice to mine
                          And thrice again, to make up nine.
                          Peace, the charm's wound up.

Enter Macbeth and Banquo

MACBETH: So foul and fair a day I have not seen.

BANQUO:	. . . What are these, So withered and so wild in their attire, That look not like the inhabitants of the earth? . . .
MACBETH:	Speak, if you can: what are you?
FIRST WITCH:	All hail, Macbeth, hail to thee, Thane of Glamis!
SECOND WITCH:	All hail, Macbeth, hail to thee, Thane of Cawdor!
THIRD WITCH:	All hail, Macbeth, that shall be king hereafter!
BANQUO:	. . . My noble partner You greet with present grace, and great prediction Of noble having and royal hope . . . To me you speak not.
FIRST WITCH:	Hail!
SECOND WITCH:	Hail!
THIRD WITCH:	Hail!
FIRST WITCH:	Lesser than Macbeth, and greater.
SECOND WITCH:	Not so happy, yet much happier.
THIRD WITCH:	Thou shalt get kings, though thou be none.
FIRST WITCH:	Banquo and Macbeth, all hail!
MACBETH:	Stay, you imperfect speakers. Tell me more . . . Speak, I charge you.
	Witches vanish.
BANQUO:	The earth hath bubbles, as the water has, And these are of them. Whither are they vanished?
MACBETH:	. . . Melted, as breath into the wind. Would they had stayed
BANQUO:	Were such things here as we do speak about? Or have we eaten on the insane root That takes the reason prisoner?!
MACBETH:	Your children shall be kings.
BANQUO:	You shall be king.

The teacher whose class acted out the opening scene encouraged her students to read the scene aloud again and again. By doing so the students became comfortable with the words and by trying the lines in a variety of ways, they got to know more about the scene and were able to identify those things that puzzled them or that they needed to know more about — this approach is advocated in working with the key scenes suggested.

Turning a scene into tableaux

To avoid having the scene played as a collection of talking heads, have the students divide the scene into four tableaux. For example, the first tableau would feature the witches; the second, Macbeth and Banquo meeting the witches; the third, the prophecy; and the fourth, Macbeth and Banquo trying to figure out what has just taken place. Play the tableaux in sequence, making the transitions from tableau to tableau in slow motion. Now, have the students read their lines as they form and transition from one tableau to the next. Doing this will ensure that the scenes have some animation. Some teachers find it useful to have the students play the scene like a silent movie with all the requisite jerky movements, exaggerated body language, and over-the-top facial expressions. Either way, these types of activities help the students to realize that the players don't just stand in one position or place when delivering lines from a script.

Presenting a scripted scene

When students have worked up their scenes, pair the groups and have them play for each other. If students want to go off script, let them; otherwise, scripts may be used. At the conclusion of the sharing, gather the class together for discussion. Ask these questions:

- How did rehearsing and presenting your scenes help you to understand the story and the characters?
- What did you enjoy about your partner group's work that you might like to incorporate into your scene?
- What did you enjoy most about rehearsing and enacting a scripted scene?

Dramatic extensions

See the Glossary, "Overview of Drama Conventions," for a summary of conventions that could be used to extend drama work.

The drama work with scripts can be extended in a number of ways, including taking it into writing. Here are some other possibilities:

- The teacher-in-role could step into a scene and interview a character about his or her unspoken thoughts. Possible inquiries: What is Macbeth really thinking as the witch tells Banquo his sons will be kings? What is going through the mind of the third witch as she listens to the prophecies?
- Using the role on the wall strategy, the class could chart character profiles, and those characters could be hot-seated. For example, after the sleepwalking scene, a whole-class interview of the Gentlewoman might take place.
- Students could write in role as a character who is not in the play but who could be. For example: A young maid who was hired on the day King Duncan was murdered writes home to a girlfriend about the terrible events in the castle, or a young waiter who was pouring wine for the guests during the banquet writes to his mother about the strange behavior of King Macbeth.
- Using the viewpoint of a character whose opinions the class doesn't know, have the students create a short monologue to be spoken aloud. Perhaps one murderer of Banquo could explain how things went wrong on the night of the slaying or a soldier in Macbeth's army could tell what he thought when he saw the forest, Birnam Wood, coming towards Macbeth's castle.

In this chapter we have journeyed through narrative, considering many strategies that enable students to experiment with ways of reading aloud. It is our belief that a lively approach to the work provides students representing a broad range of abilities with a sense of ownership and achievement.

11

Sharing Our Role-Playing

Traditionally, drama in school has been thought of in relation to a "stage presentation" — a performance at the school assembly or at a parents' night, or a play put on by a visiting group. Today, however, drama in education encompasses many kinds of activities, from Kindergarten students' play in a dress-up centre, to a professional presentation of a play written for a specific audience. The relationship between spectator and participant across the broad spectrum of drama experiences is an important aspect of drama education.

A Range of Ways to Share

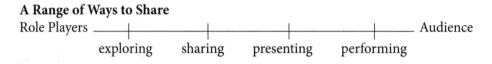

The Relationship Between Participants and Audience

The degree to which an audience matters to the work of drama participants affects the values of the work. Concerns related to audience are lowest when the focus is on exploring drama and highest when the focus is on giving a public performance.

Exploring drama

The goal of the drama lesson is to explore ideas, roles, physical and verbal interaction, feelings, and attitudes. There may be reasons for sharing, but exploration and learning come first.

Sharing drama

Sharing is the interaction that occurs when individuals or groups communicate with others. Those watching can see different interpretations of the text; can be part of a sequential sharing of the scenes from the story; or can help with work in progress, as each group takes suggestions for further exploration. Through the free exchange of ideas, students discover or clarify their assumptions, see different points of view, become aware of emotional reactions that may differ greatly from their own, and begin to understand the roles and the drama they are creating.

Although students may wish to take an activity out of the classroom environment to share it with a wider audience, the decision should be made with care. When students are placed in performance situations, the point of view of the audience becomes the major consideration, not the development of the students' own feelings and relationships — this type of sharing should occur *only* when the students are fully prepared and ready, and when the exploration and learning have been wholly satisfactory.

Presenting drama

Presenting drama involves sharing work with others who have not been engaged in the process of exploring and learning. It might involve showing the work to another class in the same school or to students engaged in similar activities but at different times and places. Since different classes work differently and have different evaluation criteria, the teachers of both spectators and participants must take this into account in any type of presentation. Some polishing and refinement may be necessary, since the emotional risks to the students are greater in more formal situations.

Performing drama

Performing is a formal event, a way of sharing dramatic work with an audience that is outside the creative process and that sees and evaluates only the finished product. Therefore, the performance must be polished and practised for the sake of the audience and the respect given to the performers. Teachers are wise to ensure that students who are growing and learning at various stages of development are not put in the high-risk position of trying to please an audience.

Much of what students do in drama in education involves sharing their role-playing, which they can do both within drama events and within certain kinds of roles.

Students can begin by sharing with an audience *within* the drama events. In this way they become both spectators and participants at the same time. The class may decide on a theme that it wants to explore and, in small groups, students prepare a short scene that expresses their views. Other groups can watch the work while it is in progress. Through sensitive side-coaching, the teacher can make suggestions and help resolve problems.

When all the groups have shaped their work, the groups can share their scenes with the rest of the class taking a type of role. For example, perhaps each group is presenting its interpretation of a crime. Those watching can role-play townspeople and decide which interpretation they think works best. Then — like a jury — they can decide on the guilt of an individual.

When weighing the value of having students share their work with others, the teacher is wise to consider the following:

- the purpose for the sharing, as well as the impact the sharing will have on the work being explored in drama
- the social health of the group, and whether the students wish to share the work (e.g., should beginners be encouraged to show work or should they concentrate on themselves and their own group?)
- the value of exploring informal ways of working with an audience (e.g., informal demonstration for discussion or observational purposes, on-the-spot spontaneous sharing during the lesson, or a sharing of work with others carrying on a similar exploration)
- the advantages and disadvantages of setting up situations where volunteers can do the sharing (e.g., an "after-four" group)
- the appropriateness of keeping an emphasis on encouraging more exploration and development of new ideas that deepen the drama

Eyewitness Angles

A retelling of the Greek myth about Daedalus and Icarus can incorporate still images, or tableaux, as representations of the story's historical framework. Tableaux are "frozen pictures" created by the students in response to a theme, situation, or story. They show movement arrested, and their use allows students to focus on one significant moment. This strategy provides opportunities for students to observe each other's work from the relative safety of the shared content or context, where everyone is engaged in representing an aspect of the theme. No one is being "stared at"; everyone is exploring the ideas being represented. In addition, students learn to contribute to a group effort and gain experience in telling stories and in presenting situations from different points of view. How much detail can they reveal in their pictures? Could the last tableau be constructed with the whole class? Could the narration be recorded by a group incorporating a music background as a soundtrack for the images? Could the images be photographed, scanned to screen, and made into a YouTube production with the narration added?

Here is text for "The Flight of Icarus," which either teacher or students can narrate while students in partners dramatize the story.

> Daedalus and his son Icarus are trapped in the labyrinth, prey to the Minotaur. Side by side, father and son move through the maze, their hands sliding along myriad walls, following endless corners. There is no way out. Gazing up, Daedalus sees a bird in flight. A feather drifts down. Freedom! Father and son begin gathering feathers and fashioning wings. Icarus slips into his wings, tests them, rises a few inches off the ground, and discovers that he can fly. Impatiently, Icarus rejoins his father, who is still binding his wings to his arms. Daedalus looks ahead to the sun, then cautiously extends his wings. With outstretched arms, father and son begin to fly — slowly, fluidly. They leave the labyrinth below; above them, the sun. They begin to feel the sun's heat melting the wax holding their wings. Daedalus draws back, but Icarus is enraptured with the power of flight. Daedalus' pleas go unheeded as Icarus soars towards the sun. Ascension. Pain. His wings disintegrate. Icarus spirals to earth.

Retelling the story from the viewpoint of one of the characters not necessarily mentioned in the story can offer students opportunities to work in narrative, and this can deepen the drama that has been constructed. Consider the possibilities for storytelling when a student adopts one of the following roles, which can be outlined on chalkboard or SMART Board:

- Reporter: *Here is what I have chosen to tell.*
- Witness: *I was there and I saw it all.*
- Neighbor: *My neighbor told me all about what happened.*
- Friend: *I need to tell you what happened to my friend.*
- Gossip: *You won't believe what I just heard.*
- Commentator: *This is the news! Today, this story is just in . . .*
- Leader: *Listen, my people! You must understand what I will tell you.*
- Rebel: *Don't believe a word of this account.*
- Judge: *I seek to uphold the law.*
- Parent: *When I was a child, this story was so important to me.*

- Therapist: *Your problems will be revealed in the story I will tell you.*
- Police officer: *Here is what happened, your honor.*
- Government bureaucrat: *This story is the official word of the government.*
- Social worker: *We must do something about the people in this report.*
- Conscience: *What fills my mind as I tell this story?*
- Alien: *How amusing. This event would not happen in my world.*
- Spokesperson: *I will tell you what has happened so that we know how to proceed.*
- Patient: *After I tell this story, you will know what happened to me.*
- Inmate: *I will tell this anecdote to fill my jail with sunshine, if only for a moment.*
- Family member: *This tale has been passed down in our family.*
- Traitor: *This is not exactly how it happened. Let me tell you.*
- Seer: *I will tell you a story and it will come true.*
- Spirit: *I want to tell you something. Can you see or hear me?*
- Coach: *Let me help you tell what happened.*
- The Chosen One: *Only I can relate what has befallen all of us.*
- Robot: *I have recorded what has happened and will play it back.*
- Artist: *I will transform the event according to my own needs.*

Invite each student to select a role from the list and prompt the students to enter the dialogue begun by this question: "Did anyone see Icarus fall?"

Students in role will need to consider questions like these: How will they connect to the event? What context will have to be determined? Will they each find a way to enter the conversation, building on previous statements? Could the drama have a contemporary setting? What would the context be for this event today, or in the future? Who could Icarus be? In that new context, who could Icarus be?

One class decided it was the Superman story and that Superman had fallen to the ground because of the "evil enemy" Sunman. They built the responses of their roles around this context.

Moving from Image into Drama

Images offer a ready starting point for drama by encouraging students to suggest ideas and ask questions. Students quickly take ownership of a visual by pointing out what they know and imagining ideas suggested by the subject matter and the artistic technique. Visuals that appeal to the imagination or that stretch students' perceptions of what they know make for the most compelling sources.

This drama lesson uses an illustration by the Canadian artist Murray Kimber. The illustration comes from a picture book, *Josepha* by Jim McGugan. It is a real-life moment frozen in time like a tableau. Take a look at the image on the next page.

Activity 1: Have the students study the picture with a talk partner. Depending on the experience of the students, the lesson could begin by having the students create their own list of questions about the illustration. Otherwise, ask them to consider the following questions:

Who are the people?
Where are they?
When is this taking place? (Modern day? Long ago?)

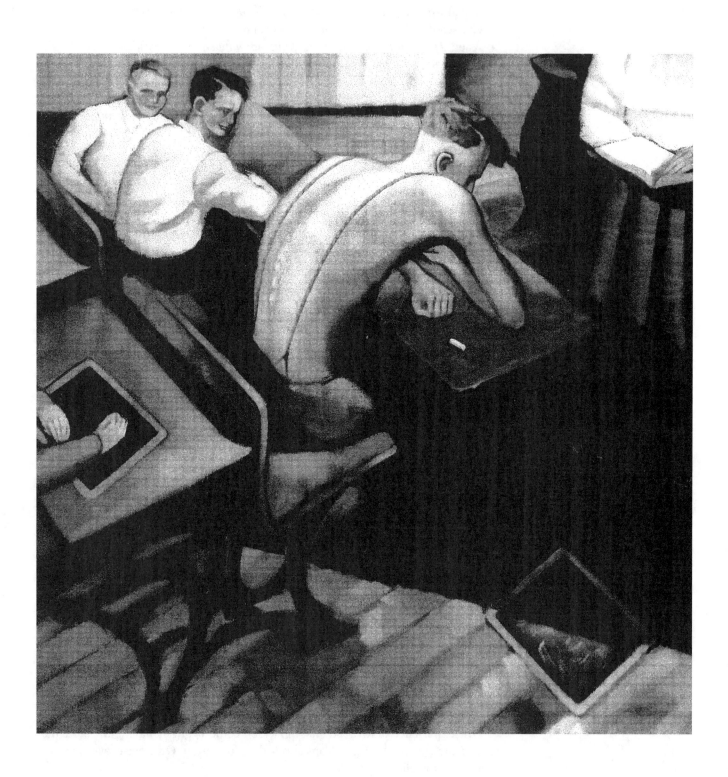

How do you know?

What sort of background are the people from?

Do you think the people know each other?

What is the general mood? How do you know?

What do you think is being said?

What do you think they were all doing five minutes ago?

What do you think will happen next?

How has the artist drawn your attention to the centre of interest?

If you were to step into the picture, where would you place yourself?

Who would you like to take with you? Why?

Augmenting Roles

In one class, there were more students than figures in the picture, so the teacher suggested that the rest of the students be in role as members of the community who had a special interest in the school.

Activity 2: Each student chooses one figure from the illustration to represent.

Have the students come into the playing space one at a time and take up their positions as per the illustration. When everyone has found a position within the tableau, have them memorize that position before dissolving it.

Divide the large tableau into a series of smaller ones. Tell the students to bring their part of the tableau to life with movement and dialogue.

When the animated sequences are ready, begin with the action at the back of the tableau and move it up to the front.

Have the students consider the overall mood in their work. What is appropriate in this context?

Creating an Anthology

An anthology is a drama event constructed with several selections chosen because they relate to a theme the class wishes to explore. An effective culminating activity based on the drama strategies the students have explored, an anthology can be presented for the school or for a parents' evening. You may want to begin with a text that the students have enjoyed and draw upon the themes within it to create an anthology, select an issue from a component in the curriculum, and have the students look for resources; alternatively, the students can suggest a theme that interests them, such as building an anthology around castles, as one class did, because of interest in the Harry Potter books. One Grade 7 class explored the role of women in Iran as part of their work on social issues and found many types of texts as resources for drama work, including the novel *The Breadwinner* by Deborah Ellis. Another class, Grade 2, found items pertaining to weather and linked them all with a weather map on screen and a weather spokesperson. The selections for drama can encompass poems, stories, events, excerpts from novels, interviews, articles, and songs.

Once the collected selections are in, each member can find and bring in material that relates to it in some significant way. The students can examine, discuss, and analyze this material, and select the pieces that they want to explore and connect through their drama work. They can decide on the order in which the material will be presented and work towards a strong beginning and ending for the anthology.

Transitions linking one selection to the next are important because they provide continuity in the anthology. Since there will not be a plot or any main characters, the focus is on the anthology showing aspects of the theme in a way that is logical or dramatically powerful. Transitions can be effectively created through movement, song, recurring statements, or improvisation. A narrator-in-role can link the items together, a guitarist or singer can provide a musical link, slides on screen can connect the items, or there can be a scenario where characters, perhaps family members, reminisce to connect the various selections.

Each selection can serve as a resource for exploring with the whole class, or after a general discussion about the nature of the dramatic anthology, the selections can be divided among the groups for dramatic exploration.

Prompt your students to consider which drama techniques they want to use to bring their selections to life. They may think of tableaux, choral speaking, storytelling, Readers Theatre, movement, dance, and dialogue. You could also direct each group to find a way to involve the rest of the class in the themed scene it develops — in that way, the class becomes an ensemble creating the performance.

One middle-school class developed an anthology around four teacher-researched poems, which appear below. The class added an urban ghost story as a link to the poems and researched other urban legends. Members presented their anthology in the basement of the school to two classes at a time, with appropriate music to set the atmosphere.

Outline of an anthology presentation — Poems of Loneliness

The class began with a Readers Theatre interpretation of the urban tale "The Foreign Hotel" and then followed with the dramatization of the four poems using a variety of drama strategies. The selections were linked with a videotape on screen of only a closeup of a student's mouth, welcoming people to this evening of events conjured up by loneliness. The voice, along with eerie background music, introduced each selection for which the title was given.

The Foreign Hotel

A Lady and her daughter were traveling abroad, and arrived late at night, very tired after an exhausting journey, at the hotel where they booked their rooms. The mother was particularly worn out. They were put into adjoining rooms, and the daughter tumbled into bed and fell asleep at once. She slept long and heavily, and it was well on in the next day before she got up. She opened the door into her mother's room, and found it empty. And it was not the room into which they have gone the night before. The wallpaper was different, the bed was made up. She rang up, and got no answer to her bell. She dressed and went downstairs.

"Can you tell me where my mother is?" she said to the woman at the reception desk.

"Your mother, mademoiselle?"

"Yes, the lady who arrived with me last night."

"But, mademoiselle, you came alone."

"We booked in; the night porter will remember; we wrote for two rooms!"

"Mademoiselle indeed wrote for two rooms, but she arrived alone."

And whenever she asked among the servants she got the same answer, until she began to think that she must be mad.

At last she went back to England and told her friends what had happened and one of them went to investigate. He went to the consul and the police and at last he found the truth. The mother had been more than tired when she arrived that night — she had been in the invasion stages of cholera. No sooner had she gone to bed than she was taken violently ill; the doctor was sent for, she died, and the hotel owners were filled with panic and decided to conceal all that happened. The body was carried away, the furniture was taken out to be burnt, the walls were re-papered, and all the staff were told to allow nothing to be guessed of what had happened. They knew that not a guest would be left to them if it became known that cholera had been in the hotel.

Commentary on "The Listeners": For the poem below, the students created a building with their bodies, becoming rooms, a staircase, and furniture. As the traveller knocked on the door and then entered the house, the students began whispering the narration, some taking solo lines, others speaking in unison. The traveller spoke his lines and eventually left. The building grew silent until the room was filled with hollow laughter.

The Listeners

'Is there anybody there?' said the Traveller,
　　Knocking on the moonlit door;
And his horse in the silence champed the grasses
　　Of the forest's ferny floor:
And a bird flew up out of the turret,
　　Above the Traveller's head:
And he smote upon the door again a second time;
　　'Is there anybody there?' he said.
But no one descended to the Traveller;
　　No head from the leaf-fringed sill
Leaned over and looked into his grey eyes,
　　Where he stood perplexed and still.
But only a host of phantom listeners
　　That dwelt in the lone house then
Stood listening in the quiet of the moonlight
　　To that voice from the world of men:
Stood thronging the faint moonbeams on the dark stair,
　　That goes down to the empty hall,
Hearkening in an air stirred and shaken
　　By the lonely Traveller's call.
And he felt in his heart their strangeness,
　　Their stillness answering his cry,
While his horse moved, cropping the dark turf,
　　'Neath the starred and leafy sky;
For he suddenly smote on the door, even
　　Louder, and lifted his head:-
'Tell them I came, and no one answered,
　　That I kept my word' he said.
Never the least stir made the listeners,
　　Though every word he spake
Fell echoing through the shadowiness of the still house
　　From the one man left awake:
Ay, they heard his foot upon the stirrup,
　　And the sound of iron on stone,
And how the silence surged softly backward,
　　When the plunging hoofs were gone.

— *Walter de la Mare*

Commentary on "Some One": For the poem below, the students began miming a variety of children's playground games. Then the members of the group that had prepared the poem gathered under a classroom table — their wee, small house. When a knocking was heard, they began speaking the poem. At the end, they all froze in place, sucking their thumbs.

Some One

Some one came knocking
  At my wee, small door;
Some one came knocking,
  I'm sure-sure-sure;
I listened, I opened,
  I looked to left and right,
But nought was there a-stirring
  In the still dark night;
Only the busy beetle
  Tap-tapping in the wall,
Only from the forest
  The screech-owl's call,
Only the cricket whistling
  While the dewdrops fall,
So I know not who came knocking,
  At all, at all, at all.

— *Walter de la Mare*

Commentary on "The Frozen Man": The group that presented the last poem divided the poem into individual lines, which they spoke in a monotone. They dressed in hooded sweatshirts with flashlights shining up on their faces. They kept moving towards those watching and shouted the last three lines: "Let him in . . ."

The Frozen Man

Out at the edge of town
where black trees

crack their fingers
in the icy wind

and hedges freeze
on their shadows

and the breath of cattle,
still as boulders,

hangs in rags
under the rolling moon,

a man is walking
alone:

on the coal-black road
his cold

feet
ring

and
ring.

Here in a snug house
at the heart of town

the fire is burning
red and yellow and gold:

you can hear the warmth
like a sleeping cat

breathe softly
in every room.

When the frozen man
comes to the door,

let him in,
let him in,
let him in.

— *Kit Wright*

The sharing of the drama concluded with all of the students moving towards an audience member or two, with each player whispering another urban tale to the listeners, until the teacher began ringing an old school bell, the signal for the end of the anthology presentation.

Building an Ensemble Drama

Ensemble drama is a production created by a large group from a single source that provides opportunities for involving the whole class and using a variety of drama forms. Almost any source can be used to develop an ensemble drama, but folk tales, with their strongly patterned plots, wide variety of fascinating characters, and spare colorful language, make good starting points. We like compressed retellings of folk tales because they readily enable us to add our own drama explorations. In an ensemble drama, the large group is divided into small groups, each developing a different form of presentation — choral speaking, movement and dance, rituals and ceremonies, improvised scenes, and sound exploration or music being among the most common.

Once the source has been shared (see the sample text, "The Reindeer Herder and the Moon," pages 136 to 138), students choose the presentation form they would like to explore. The teacher will need to ensure that students spread themselves reasonably among the presentation choices. For example, a choral speaking group of two voices will be less effective than one with five or more voices. Designating the maximum number of students required for each group is useful.

Group work requires at least 45 minutes to an hour. In some cases, it may benefit the students to work together on each presentation form and then select the one they will concentrate on for the performance.

When the groups assemble to put the pieces together, remind the students that they are working with a living text. A script might eventually emerge but for the moment, improvisation is the way forward. Each group could present its contribution before any decision is made about a precise order, or a rough sequence could be suggested and then refined as desired. The aim is not to retell the plot as much as it is to capture the essence or spirit of the tale, for example, a magical journey.

Once the large group sees what it has, invite the students to consider it critically. Have them identify where more material might be needed (e.g., by asking whether the movement section needs to be extended) and suggest how transitions can be smoothed and where aspects of group work can be combined. For example, could the sound exploration and music group accompany the movement and dance segment? Encourage the students to experiment and explore the possibilities of the work rather than settling quickly on one idea.

Above all, co-operation and sharing comprise the overarching goal as the students strive to listen to and respect the ideas generated among them, and support, sustain, and strengthen their collective creation.

Devising ensemble drama based on "The Reindeer Herder and the Moon"

The following suggestions call for the creation of four groups: one focused on choral speaking, one on sound exploration, one on movement, and one on improvisation. All use a traditional story, "The Reindeer Herder and the Moon," as source. The story features a reindeer with magical powers and explains how out of his love for a young reindeer herder, Moon got his phases. Instructions for each of the presentation forms should be printed on cards for each group. The order in which the groups present does not matter.

Choral speaking: "Your place is here in the heavens."
Create a choral speaking piece in which the stars warn Moon not to venture anywhere near Earth.
1. Make a list poem out of possible consequences for Moon if he leaves his world to travel to Earth. Example:
      Your light will dim.
      Your body will fade . . .
2. Determine how to match text with voices. Use lots of solos in the piece and create a group chorus, which can be repeated at intervals. Example of chorus:
      You mustn't go down.
      You mustn't go down.
      Your place is here with us.

Sound exploration/Music: "He became their nightly beacon."
Canadian composer F. Murray Schafer has devised this activity for students.
1. Create as many suggestive words for "moonlight" as you can.
      Examples: oomooloo, lumoona
      In your group, select three or four of these new words from the list and explore the sound possibilities for each. Produce the most richly textured sound you can by exploring pitch (range from high to low), rate (fast, slow), and volume (loud/soft). The combination of these elements should produce many possibilities.
2. When each word has been explored thoroughly, arrange your new sound pieces in a pleasing pattern. The group might also sustain some sounds softly

while bringing in other sounds over them. The addition of a few bells might be introduced towards the end of the composing.

Movement: "I can transform you into something else."
By means of magical transformation, the reindeer protects the girl.
By means of Earth's gravity, Moon loses his ability to float gracefully and becomes clumsy and awkward.
Because of a promise he must make, Moon will have to transform his shape on a regular basis for all time.

1. Working with the idea of transformation, create a movement piece that explores the characters, issues, and ideas of the story.
2. The students could begin in pairs. Student A begins by creating a still shape of the reindeer herder. Student B adds to this shape by creating a new shape. Student A breaks away, perhaps in a spiraling motion, and creates a new shape. Student B moves to student A and makes a new shape. The pairs might think about magical transformations and improvise until they have a short piece.
3. The phases of the moon could also be the subject of improvisation. In order to explore the changes that overcame Moon when he reached Earth, the whole group, one member at a time, could come forward and create the shape of Moon at the peak of his powers. One by one, other group members join in. Once the sculpture has been formed, it disintegrates in slow motion; then, in slow motion, one person at a time, the group creates other kinds of moons, such as a struggling moon, a diminished moon, a defeated moon, a captured moon, and a resurrected moon.
4. An order can be worked out for the whole composition, and the group can put it together. The group members should be encouraged to employ different levels, tempos, qualities (e.g., heavy, light, smooth, clumsy), body movements (e.g., stretching, twisting, and pushing), and ways to use the space.

Improvisation: "So, Moon Man, I have captured you."
This task involves students in creating a series of short monologues in which explanations are given about Moon's reckless journey to Earth by different eyewitnesses, such as the reindeer, a star, and the reindeer herder.

1. Have students work in pairs and compile a list of five or six questions that could be used by a reporter to interview one of the eyewitnesses.
   Sample Questions for the Reindeer Herder:
   > When you saw Moon climbing down, what were your first thoughts?
   > You seemed afraid of Moon at first, then suddenly you became bold and taunted him. What brought about the change?
   > He made promises to you. What has worked? What hasn't worked?
2. Within student pairs, have the students take on the roles of a reporter and the story character for whom they have prepared questions. Ask the interviewers to jot down the answers that the interviewees give during the interviews. Halfway through the questions, have the students switch roles.
3. Prompt the students to use their answers to the questions to create a list poem of six lines. Encourage them to choose the most interesting answer as their opening line. Next, look for a good second line. Choose the closing line next, then fill in the middle. The students are allowed to rephrase, edit, or change comments they jotted down during the interview. Remind the

students that they will be speaking in the first person and that they need to be consistent throughout.

4. Student pairs can now practise their monologue orally. Since it was shaped by two people, it can be spoken by two voices in unison, or in any other way that sounds pleasing.

Here is the full text of the story that provides the basis for the group work outlined above.

The Reindeer Herder and the Moon

Moon was lonely.

He had fallen in love with a young reindeer herder on the earth beneath, and he couldn't stop thinking about her.

"Put her out of your mind," warned the stars. "She belongs on Earth. Your place is here in the heavens shining along with the rest of us."

But Moon paid no attention. He dreamed of having the girl by his side.

One night, as he watched her returning to her camp on the back of a large reindeer, he was overcome by a powerful urge to fetch her. So he started to climb down.

At first the girl didn't see him. Then she looked up. "How close the moon appears!" she said. She raised her hand to shield her eyes from his brightness, and that's when she saw his long spindly leg and skinny arms. The sight of him was terrifying.

"Oh!" she cried. "The Moon Man is coming for me! What can I do?"

Her reindeer turned and spoke. "Jump from my back. I'll dig a hole in the snow where you can hide."

With his powerful hind legs the reindeer kicked a hollow in the snow. The girl jumped in and the reindeer pushed snow all around her, leaving only the top of her white fur hood uncovered. Then the reindeer moved into the distance.

Moon stepped onto the earth. His narrow spindly legs felt very strange beneath the weight of his body. He looked from side to side. He had expected to see the herder and her reindeer. He had not expected to see an empty landscape.

"Where is she?" muttered Moon. "She was here only moments ago."

Even as he spoke he was practically standing on top of her. Then he spied reindeer tracks in the snow. He started to follow them, but soon thought better of the idea. He wasn't used to walking about like this. A heavy feeling came over him. His light had dimmed considerably.

"She's run off," sighed Moon. "I'd better turn back." With great difficulty, Moon started to climb back into the sky.

The higher he climbed the brighter he became. The higher he climbed the stronger he felt. Soon he floated easily among the stars.

On earth, the reindeer dug the girl from the snow. She leapt onto his back and made haste to her camp.

Suddenly Moon looked down and saw her. This time he didn't climb out of the sky. He plunged instantly toward the earth.

The reindeer saw him coming.

"Moon is returning!" he shouted.

"I must hide!" cried the girl. "Where?"

"I can hide you," said the reindeer. "With my magic powers I can transform you into something else. You could become a tent pole."

"No, said the girl. "He might crush the tent."

"You could become one of the skins on the sleeping platform."

"He could carry that off," replied the girl.

The reindeer looked about hurriedly.

"I have it!" he said. "I can change you into an oil lamp. In the glare of Moon's brightness you will not be seen."

And that's what Reindeer did. He struck his front hoof three times on the surface of the snow, and where the girl had stood there now appeared a stone oil lamp burning with a tiny bright flame.

Reindeer hid as Moon picked his way uncertainly toward the tent.

"Where are you?" he cried. He reached out, lifted the flap and peered in.

"Where are you hiding?" he demanded. "Are you under the sleeping platform?"

He raised the sleeping platform. No one was hiding there.

"Are you behind the tent pole?"

He peeked behind the tent pole. No one was hiding there.

"Are you under the cooking pot?"

He lifted the cooking pot. No one was hiding there.

All the time he looked, the tiny flame fluttered and danced in the Arctic night.

Moon withdrew from the tent. He was baffled. "How does she disappear like that?" he wondered.

"Where does she go?"

There was a giggle from inside the tent. Moon tore open the tent flap and barged inside. No one was there. Only the tiny lamp flame leapt and whirled in the sudden breeze Moon had made as he entered.

Moon stumbled outside. He did not feel well. A great heaviness had come over him. His light was nearly out.

"The stars were right," thought Moon. "I've no business being down here." He was about to leave when a peal of laughter rang out! Moon turned. The girl had regained her shape and was peering at him from behind the tent flap.

"Here I am!" she taunted.

Moon lurched toward her, tripped over his feet and crashed to the snow.

The girl was on him in a flash. She threw the reindeer harness around his legs, pulled it tight and shouted, "So, Moon Man, I have captured you."

But Moon said nothing. His teeth chattered violently. His light was almost gone. He appeared completely helpless. When he did speak, his voice came in a whisper.

"Please! Please help me! Unfasten my legs. Let me return to the skies."

"And if I do, you will grow strong again and come chasing after me," said the girl.

"No, never!" cried the moon. "I shall never come down from the skies again. Please release me and I will reward you and all your people."

"And what reward would that be, Moon Man?"

Moon's voice was so weak that the girl had to put her ear right up to his lips to listen. When he finished speaking, her face beamed.

She leapt to her feet, whistled to her reindeer and freed Moon's legs. Then she slipped the harness under Moon's arms and tossed one end to the reindeer. He gripped it in his teeth, and while she pushed from behind, the reindeer pulled.

Slowly, slowly Moon rose to his feet. He put one arm around the girl and the other over the reindeer's back and took a few halting steps. Then he started to climb back into the sky.

Higher and higher he climbed.

Brighter and brighter he became.

Soon Moon had regained his rightful place among the stars.

True to his word, Moon rewarded the girl and her people. He became their nightly beacon, guiding them across the frozen Arctic lands. He became their calendar, measuring their year for them.

He became for her people
The Moon of the Old Bull
The Moon of the Birth of Calves
The Moon of the Waters.
He became
The Moon of Leaves
The Moon of Warmth
The Moon of the Shedding of Antlers.
He became
The Moon of Love Among the Wild Deer
The Moon of the First Winter
The Moon of the Shortening Days.
And true to his word, Moon never came down to Earth again.

From *Little Book of Northern Tales: The Bear Says North* by Bob Barton

Games and Activities

Games and warm-up activities can serve many functions in the classroom. Sometimes they are all about students getting to know one another. They can also be useful in developing concentration and awareness, promoting idea finding, and building teamwork.

The Apple Tree

Students enter the pretend world of the game in the knowledge that they must play by the rules. The rules for deciding who will be It in a game is often a game itself, as illustrated in this counting-out ritual.

Everyone forms a circle. A volunteer goes to the centre of the circle, covers his or her eyes with one hand, and points with the other. Players in the circle chant the following verse as the player in the middle turns slowly:

> When I went up the apple tree,
> All the apples fell on me,
> Bake a pudding, bake a pie,
> Did you ever tell a lie?
> Yes, you did,
> You know you did.
> You broke your mother's teapot lid,
> L-I-D spells "lid"
> And out goes you!

When the chant ends, the student in the middle stops turning, and whoever is pointed at is It for whatever game is to follow.

Little Sally Walker

This old game, originally called Little Sally Saucer, has changed significantly since the 1960s. What used to involve a bit of mime and minimal movement has become a fast-paced, dance-like game filled with fun and laughter. You can watch many examples on www.youtube.com.

The players form a circle (with any number of participants) and a volunteer enters the circle strutting, prancing, or skipping about as the others clap hands and chant:

> Little Sally Walker
> Walking down the street
> Didn't know what to do
> So she stopped in front of me.

On the words "stopped in front of me," the player inside the circle stops and faces another player and performs a movement motif, such as jump-jump-full turn, as the other players chant.

139

Hey, girl, do this thing.
Do this thing and switch.

The two players quickly switch places, and the new player repeats the movement motif as the rest continue chanting:

Hey, girl, do this thing.
Do this thing and switch.

The new player now moves off to engage another player as the group chants:

Little Sally Walker
Walking down the street
Didn't know what to do
So she stopped in front of me.

Dusty Bluebells

This game is a bit like Follow the Leader with an incantation. You can watch the game played on www.youtube.com to learn the tune.

Have the players form a circle of arches by joining hands and holding them up. Select a player to be It and have that player weave through the arches while the other players sing:

In and out the dusty bluebells
In and out the dusty bluebells
In and out the dusty bluebells
Who shall be my partner?

When the song stops, the player who is It stands behind a player in the circle, taps the player on the shoulder, and sings along with the group:

Tippity tappety on your shoulder
Tippity tappety on your shoulder
Tippity tappety on your shoulder
You shall be my partner.

The tapped player detaches from the arches, links on to the shoulders of the student who is It, and the game continues. As the arches grow fewer and the line grows longer, things can become a little muddled and a lot of fun.

Under the Water (with Teacher-as-Narrator)

The teacher uses voice-over narration while the students create the activity. The students must, therefore, listen carefully to know what to do and when to do it. This activity provides a built-in control, allowing the teacher to give the cues for the drama while the students explore their own ideas. Eventually, the students may serve as their own narrators.

Although the narrator tells the participants *what* to do, *how* to do it is left up to the students. In this way, opportunities for unique, personal, and creative decisions are incorporated into the activity.

Narration:

"You are on a boat ready to search for a ship, laden with treasure, which sank 300 years ago near these rocks. The islanders warn of dangers. What might these be? How can you avoid them? Choose a partner so that you can always dive in pairs. . . . Because you are using oxygen cylinders, the mouthpiece makes it necessary to arrange a sign language for communicating with your partner. Each pair must decide what to take down: knife, rope, flashlight, harpoon, and so on. You have two minutes to work out signs and equipment. . . . Put on rubber suits, flippers, and oxygen equipment. . . . Test your mouthpiece. . . . Put on your mask. . . . Switch on oxygen . . . and dive in.

"You are lying at the bottom of the sea in the soft green water. . . . There are rocks on the sea bed — look at them, see their shapes. There is a fish swimming around the rocks. Watch it move. It is moving away . . . getting smaller . . . and smaller. It's gone. Everything is quiet and still. Feel the sea around you. Slowly stand up.

"At every movement feel the pressure of the water. Start to move slowly . . . slowly. Explore around the rocks. What can you see? Look. If you find anything, just examine it and put it back. Remember where it is.

"Remember to move slowly to avoid stirring up sand. . . . Listen, under water, for the sound of the drum to call you back aboard. The drum is a warning that sharks have been sighted. Don't panic, but come at once to the surface, still moving slowly. Stay with your partner. Keep breathing. Ssh-ssh-ssh."

Showing Treasure: While sitting in a circle, the students can, in turn, reveal the items they saw underwater through mime and movement. The class can try to determine what the partners have discovered under the sea.

Moulding Statues

- *Moulding in Pairs:* The players choose partners. With eyes closed, player A stands still, but relaxed. Player B moulds player A, as though he or she were a lump of clay, into a statue. Neither player may speak during the game. When finished, player B walks around and looks at the other statues that have also just been made. As a result, player B may consider changing something about his or her statue. There is an opportunity to do this before the players switch roles.
- *Thrown into Position:* Any number of players can participate. One player is designated the Puller. The other players line up facing the Puller and hold out one arm. A theme for the action is decided upon. For example, if the players to be thrown are to represent members of a soccer team, each player must land in a fitting dramatic position. Common themes include scariest, ugliest, and funniest positions.
- *Cumulative Freeze:* Divide into small groups. One student makes a shape and freezes. (Advise students to choose positions that can be maintained without discomfort.) A second student finds a way, with movement and sound, to use the first student's shape, and the two students freeze in the resulting position.

A third student uses their combined shape, and all three freeze. Repeat the process until everybody is part of the freeze.

Impromptu Tableaux

The class divides into groups of 8 to 12. One student in each group is chosen to be the leader. Each group is given its own space within the classroom. Now the members of each group move around energetically in several directions like a crowd on a busy downtown street.

At any time a leader may call out a word. In response, group members freeze, forming a tableau which in some way reflects or illustrates the word. Encourage students to use a wide variety of stage positions, levels — for example, kneeling, lying down, and stretching upward — and gestures. Advise them not to be finicky about composing the picture, but to supply enough individual variety for an interesting tableau to occur.

As an example, if the leader calls "Homework!", students would quickly assume positions that embody the idea of homework. An individual student's position may or may not relate to another student's position. For example, one student might appear to be reading silently; another might appear to be reading aloud to another student, who, in turn, might seem puzzled or be taking notes. The tableau is held for about five seconds. The teacher then releases the group, and members again move about until another key word is called. This process is repeated several times, with students responding to a new key word each time.

Since the object is to form an overall picture, students must be aware of the group as a whole while they are displaying their individual reactions. If someone were to come unsuspectingly into the room, that person should be able to look at the tableau and find it quite easy to guess the key word or idea.

Who Am I?

Here are two group activities that involve students in figuring out who they are supposed to be based on spoken clues.

Characters in Conversation: Each player represents a character well known to the group, perhaps an actor or an athlete. The players do not know who they are representing, however. The identities of the characters are revealed on slips of paper, each pinned on a player's back. The players move about and talk to one another to discover through yes-and-no questions who they are.

Interviewing for a Job: One player leaves the room, then the group chooses a job for which to interview the person. One example is being a sailor with Christopher Columbus. When the group has decided, the person outside the room returns for an interview not knowing what the job is. The group then asks questions — for example, "Do you get seasick?" Interviewers must give hints, but should not give the game away. The person being interviewed answers the questions as though in an interview. When the group thinks that the interviewee has figured out what the job is, they can offer the job. The interviewee then replies, indicating that he or she knows the answer: "Yes, I would like to be a sailor on Columbus's ship" or "No, I would not like to be a sailor on Columbus's ship."

Family Stories for Drama

These stories can be used as the basis for explorations of heritage drama.

The Hungry Alligator

Many, many years ago, when my grandfather was still alive, he used to work in the canals near the sugar cane fields in Guyana. He and his partner used to work very hard cleaning the weeds and grass out of the canals.

No people lived back in and around the hills, and there was no access to transportation or anything else. So every morning, trucks would come around to take everyone to work and then, take them all back home in the evening.

One day, my grandfather went to work with the other men as usual. He worked all day and when it was almost time to go home, he was given a small area in the canal to clean out, and was attacked by an alligator. The rest of the men pulled him out, while the angry alligator pranced around. My poor grandfather nearly died that day. He was bleeding a lot from all his wounds. When the truck arrived, he was taken to hospital.

Grandfather couldn't walk for weeks and he was scared for a long time from his experience, but he was thankful to be still alive.

— Sandy, Grade 4

Coming to Canada

My mom and I came to Canada because back in Vietnam we were poor and because my aunt, uncle, grandmother, and grandfather lived in Canada. My mom swore that if she could make it ever to Canada she would cut her hair off and be bald.

It all started when my mom, aunt, and uncle and I left Vietnam on a boat. There were a lot of people, about 40, so we had to eat less. When we got onto the ocean there were storms and lightning. At the time I was only two years old. My aunt and uncle thought they were going to die. My uncle got a rope so he, my mom, my aunt and I could tie our hands together so that if we died and floated to land people would bury us together.

But the next morning, the storm and lightning stopped. We were so happy that we hadn't died. We went to Singapore, and we were separated from my aunt and uncle. We lived there for a while. Then the people from Canada came to test people to see if they knew how to speak English, but my mom failed. They sent

Pembroke Publishers ©2012 *This Book Is Not About Drama* by Myra Barrs, Bob Barton, David Booth ISBN 978-1-55138-269-2 us to the Philippines. My mom and I stayed there for four years. By then, my mom had my two-year-old brother and a sister, just born.

Soon after, the people from Canada came again. This time my mom passed the English test and they sent us to Canada. The church people took care of us. They gave us food and clothing. They asked if we wanted to live in a church in Mississauga. My mom said no because by then my aunt, uncle, grandmother and grandfather lived in Toronto. She wanted to be near them. The people helped us to get a house to live in because we didn't have a father and this is where we live now.

— *Van Quan, Grade 7*

My Grandfather

My granddad was born on May 11, 1891, in Canton, China. He came to this country by boat and landed in Victoria, British Columbia, on January 22, 1911. He came here with his brother in search of a new life.

Life was tough for the two brothers. And life became tougher when they had to pay the Head Tax to legally stay in Canada. In 1923 that amounted to a lot of money. Granddad met his first wife, who was a nanny for a rich family also from China. His first wife passed away at a very young age in Montreal.

Granddad and his brother moved from city to city in the laundry business. They had a business in Vancouver, Montreal, Toronto, and Ottawa. Many Chinese people started in the laundry business because it didn't take much money to start. This was before machines, so all it took was hard work, soap, and water.

Granddad was lonely for a long time because Chinese men were not allowed to sponsor families to come to Canada because of the Chinese Expulsion Act. This Act was not changed until the early 1950s. In 1954, Granddad went to Hong Kong to visit and meet my grandmom there. They got married in 1955. They came back to Canada and shortly after, they settled in Ottawa and Toronto and eventually moved to northern Ontario. They lived in Kirkland Lake and Kapuskasing and eventually Hornpayne, where he was in the restaurant business servicing mining communities.

My dad was born in Hearst, Ontario, because Hornpayne was so small and there was no hospital. They later moved to Toronto when Granddad retired in his early 70s. He lived in Toronto until he died in 1996 at 104 years of age.

— *Ciara, Grade 4, as told by her family*

Pembroke Publishers ©2012 *This Book Is Not About Drama* by Myra Barrs, Bob Barton, David Booth ISBN 978-1-55138-269-2

My Uncle

One day my uncle was walking on a bridge. Suddenly he fell in to the lake. Then he went home in wet clothes.

The next day he was sick. My grandma saw my uncle lying on the bed, so my grandma went to get medicine.

At night, my grandma dreamed that my uncle stepped on a skull when he fell in the lake. In the morning, my grandma knew that a person who had died in the lake didn't forgive him, so she went to the place where my uncle fell. She brought fruit and she put the fruit on a plate. Then she kneeled down and begged that person not to make my uncle sick.

— *Anh, Grade 6*

The Water Ghost

A long time ago, back in my country when I was two or three years old, my dad was a fisherman. One day my dad went out onto the ocean with my eighth oldest uncle and my tenth oldest uncle. I don't know what they were doing, but they were not fishing. My dad was in the ocean doing something when a water ghost tried to drown him. A water ghost is a spirit of someone who died in the water. My uncle helped my dad, and he survived.

— *Thinh, Grade 8*

The Dust Bowl

Here is the text used as source in "Authorities on the Story," in Chapter 9.

On Sunday morning, the wind blew outside the kitchen window. Matthew wiped the dust from his cereal bowl. He was used to removing the fine coating from everything in the house. It was almost as dusty inside as out. From the sideboard, the pictures of his mother and his grandma smiled at him.

When his father and his grandpa joined him at the table, they didn't say much, but he knew what they were thinking. Finally, he blurted out, "We aren't going to sell the farm, are we?"

His father set down his coffee mug and looked at Matthew's grandpa. "How much longer can we last, Pop?"

"As long as it takes," Grandpa answered.

"But the crops won't make it this year," his father snapped. "Without rain there'll be no grain. Without grain, there'll be no money."

Matthew said nothing. His grandpa stood up and walked over to the window. "The rain will come. The wheat will grow. It's not as bad as the last drought."

Matthew's father pushed his chair back angrily and went outside. He began to work in the small garden below the porch.

Matthew's grandpa sat down again, put milk and sugar in his tea and began to talk.

"When your grandma and I first farmed this land, we were young. We thought we had discovered gold in those fields of waving wheat. The world needed wheat, and we wanted to grow enough of it for everyone.

"We ploughed up all our land, even the field that we had decided not to seed yet. We borrowed from the bank and bought new equipment so we could plant as much wheat as possible. The prairies became a one-crop country.

"We needed luck, and the first year we found it. All the farmers did. The sun shone when it was supposed to, there was enough rain, the pests stayed away and the frost was late. Matthew, the prairies were covered with wheat.

"How fast things change on a farm! Just the next year, in mid-June, the crops were green and growing. But by July, the heat had burnt them down to nothing. When the sun took control it baked the land, and what rain there was could not soak into the ground. It was hot enough to fry your shoes. Too hot to work in the day, too hot to sleep at night. We harvested what we could, but your grandma and I began to worry.

"Then the rain stopped completely and times got worse. A hot sucking wind began to feed on the bare soil, and it blew the earth away. The grass that had fed the buffalo for centuries was no more.

"That wind blew for two solid weeks, blowing from the four corners of the world, blowing the land out from under our feet. It was the Big Dry. You had to see it to believe it Matthew. It turned our world into a dust bowl. It blew open doors, broke windows and even flattened a barn or two.

"The dirt and the dust were everywhere. Your grandma stuffed towels in the crack at the bottom of the door to keep the dust out. When I went outside, I had to put a dish towel soaked in water over my nose and mouth. The dust drifted like snow against our fences, and even buried them sometimes. Students had to walk to school backwards to keep the wind-blown soil from stinging their faces. And when they got home, they had to clean the dust out of the nostrils of the cattle.

"And, oh, the dust clouds. How I remember them. Brown ones, red ones, yellow ones, made from the soil of thousands of farms across the prairies. One big dust cloud blocked out for days. As it moved across the country it covered the land in darkness. We had to keep the lanterns lighted all day. Some people in the cities thought the end of the world had come.

"Your grandma could never get the laundry white. The curtains and the sheets were as grey as the sky. She scrubbed her fingers to the bone, but the dust kept winning. That's why we called those years the Dirty Thirties. Didn't beat your grandma, though. She fought the heat. She fought the wind. She fought the drought. Somehow she knew that she would see crops covering the fields with green again and the snow-white sheets billowing on the clothesline like great prairie schooners.

"A few of us farmers ploughed deep furrows around the fields to stop the earth from blowing away. Others thought it was hopeless to keep planting because their ploughs just turned up dry, fine dust that blew away in the wind. A few went to church and prayed for rain. For some, farming was becoming a slow way to starve."

Through the window, Matthew saw his father beginning to weed the little garden that his mother had planted before she died.

"I'm not saying we didn't consider giving up too, but we stayed. Things got better for a time, but wouldn't you know, two years later we were hit by nature one more time.

"Another cloud covered us — grasshoppers. They could black out the sun. Millions of them would stop all at once on a farm. They ate a crop in minutes, devouring every scrap of greenness. They even ate the bristles on the broom and the halter on the horse. When a train tried to run on tracks covered with grasshoppers, the wheels could get no traction, and they just spun around. Those insects could stop a train.

"The winter was the last straw for many farmers. It was colder than anyone could remember. We brought our mattresses into the kitchen at night to be near the heat of the cook-stove. The roads were so deep with snow that we couldn't go into town. We were cut off from everyone and everything.

"When many of my friends heard stories about the lush pickings on the west coast, they quit their farms. Tough farmers though they were, they left with their wives and kids, drained by heat and wind and cold and hardship. Chickens and everything else they owned were tied on the backs of the jalopies. Families were on the move. Schools were closed. The buildings were abandoned for good.

"Your father was born that year. We would put him on the bed between us and listen to the long whistles of the trains at night, heading west. I always loved that sound. Escape. We knew the trains were carrying farmers away from their land forever. But we couldn't leave, Matthew, we just couldn't leave. Some people's lives had dried up and blown away. But we stayed on our land and hung on to what little soil was left.

"Two years later, our land was alive again. It was green as far as the eye could see. The drought was over. The grasshoppers were gone. We were still farmers." His grandpa paused for a few moments. "That was fifty years ago, and the farm is still here. I could never have managed on my own after I lost your grandma, but your parents kept it going."

"Grandpa, is the Big Dry back?"

"I don't know, Matthew. I don't know."

They both stared out the window. The wind whistled, and swirls of dust danced across the fields.

Matthew went outside. His father put down the hoe, climbed the steps and sat beside him on the porch. They both stared at the bluest of skies. "I love this farm, Matthew. Your mother loved it too. She was afraid to live here at first, afraid of the space and all the quiet. But when she planted her garden, she became a part of this farm. She belonged here. You do too."

Matthew took his father's hand. "Will we have to sell the farm, Dad?"

Grandpa called out through the screen door, "The rain will come. If not this year, then next year. We can hang on."

— *David Booth*

Glossary

Overview of Drama Conventions

Overview of Drama Conventions

Drama conventions are practices and forms of representation that are widely accepted for use in drama instruction. When structuring drama lessons, a teacher chooses from a wide palette of these conventions or techniques to help students explore meaning and deepen understanding.

A Day in the Life   Students explore the experience of a character by working backwards from a significant moment or turning point in that person's life to build the story that accounts for the event. Students work in groups, drawing on use of tableaux, improvisation, and role play, to depict key moments that may have occurred within the 24-hour period before the significant moment in the character's life. The scenes are then presented in chronological sequence.

Alter Ego   Students work in pairs, one as the role player, the other as that role player's thoughts and feelings. The role player handles the action and dialogue, while the alter ego plays out the inner conscience and subconscious.

Carousel   After rehearsing a short performance piece within a drama, small groups can present their work without interruption. The teacher numbers the groups and directs student that everyone will remain still and silent until it is their group's turn to perform. Usually, an order is given for the groups to present. Using slow motion, counting silently in their heads for five seconds, or signaling to freeze the work can help enhance the performances, which usually last less than one minute each.

Ceremony   A ceremony is a formal act or set of formal acts established by custom or authority as part of a special occasion, such as a wedding or religious rite. Students can develop their own ceremonies as part of a drama lesson where words, songs, dance, and movement represent an invented scenario that has the effect of appearing as a ceremony.

Choral Speaking and Dramatization   Students read aloud dramatic texts such as poems by assigning parts among group members. By working with peers to read aloud poems on a particular theme or topic, or by a single poet, students take part in a creative activity that involves experimentation with voice, sound, gesture, and movement. Because of these variations, no two oral interpretations of a single poem are alike. Choral dramatization enhances students' skills of reading aloud and presentation. More important, however, is that when students work in small groups to read aloud together, their problem-solving skills are likely to be enriched as they make decisions on the best way to present.

Circular Theatre   The large group is organized into small groups, each focusing on a central character. The groups each create short improvisations that reveal the character's relationships with other characters. Then, the large group gathers in a circle, and the teacher approaches one group and signals members to play their scene. The teacher can turn away and approach another group as the former group fades out. The teacher continues in this fashion, sampling scenes, going back to revisit scenes already played in order to connect emerging story threads. Sometimes, the teacher improvises with a group in role. The students hear snippets of conversation from a variety of viewpoints and discover a broader range of possibilities for thinking about the main characters.

Collective Role   More than one person simultaneously assumes one role. Any one of the participants can speak as the character being portrayed. A character can also be improvised by a group of students, any one of whom can speak as that character. Alternatively, one student volunteers to take on the role, and the other group participants whisper advice and offer lines of dialogue to be spoken by the volunteer. In this way, a large group can be involved in the creation of a dialogue with, for instance, subgroups taking on responsibility for each of the characters in focus.

Corridor of Voices/Conscience Alley   Members of the class stand in two facing lines, thereby forming an alley. The teacher (or student) in role represents a protagonist from the drama. As the character walks slowly down the alley, the students represent the character's conscience to show his or her thoughts about making a choice. The voice can offer advice, warnings, questions, or quotations from the drama. As the character reaches the end of the alley, he or she decides what course of action to take.

Cross-Cutting   Students devise and rehearse two or more scenes, which occur at different times and in separate places. The teacher and the groups then work on cutting backwards and forwards between the two scenes, editing them to maximize the links, comparisons, analogies, similarities, or ironic contradictions between the two.

Dance Drama   Dance drama involves movement to interpret a piece of music, a series of sounds, a story, a dream, or an emotional theme. The conflict or issues inspired by a drama context are conveyed through the patterns and rhythms of dance. Dance drama can be incorporated into games, myths, legends, ceremonies, rituals, and improvised drama units.

Defining Space   Students use available material and furniture to define a space where a drama is happening. A room, a garden, a factory, a jail cell, and a restaurant are examples of sets that can be designed to physically represent places where events have taken place or settings that are talked about in the drama. The objects can be symbolic, such as a platform acting as a ship.

Documentaries   Preparing a documentary allows students to examine a theme, issue, or story from different viewpoints using a variety of drama conventions. As students work in groups to plan and prepare a documentary, they come to understand the power of using the media to inform or persuade audiences about a topic or issue.

Drawing, Graphing, and Mapping   Visuals can be used with a variety of resources, including biographies, poems, and books. Students can compare their retellings with those completed by their classmates. In collective drawing, the class or small groups make an image to represent a place or people in the drama; the image then becomes a concrete reference for ideas being discussed. Maps or diagrams made inside the drama can represent obstacles to overcome, distance to travel, or aids to problem solving; after the drama, they can be a means of reviewing or reflecting on the work.

Enactment   The plot, action, and movement in a story are dramatized as implied or described by the lines. Students can use this technique to work with a text or a story as a stimulus for dramatic exploration, or as a prepared event to be used within the drama.

Eyewitness   A student or groups of students are assigned the role of eyewitnesses to a scene. An eyewitness might be a partial or an impartial observer who remains unnoticed by those in the scene as it is happening. Eyewitnesses can report back afterwards on what they have witnessed; they should be prepared to answer questions about what they saw.

Flashback and Flash-Forward   This convention is used to provide different perspectives on the action in a drama. Scenes can be explored from an earlier point of time (flashback) to explain the causes of an action in the present. Students can also show an action in a later time by considering its imagined or actual outcome (flash-forward).

Forum Theatre   The group collaboratively explores options or possible outcomes in order to shape a dramatic scene. A dramatic situation is improvised by a small group while the rest of the class observes. Students are encouraged to participate in creating the scene by taking part in discussion, by stopping the scene to make suggestions for action or conversation, or by taking over key roles.

Freeze Frame   A moment in a drama is held still on the command "freeze." The result is a freeze frame which has not been planned in advance like a tableau or still image.

Games   Drama games and activities that generate movement, co-operation, and participation can be used in all aspects of drama learning — they formalize human interaction processes. As in drama, the players are constantly reversing roles — chasing or being chased, leading or following, shouting or listening — all of which promotes understanding of social actions and counteractions.

Groups   Children work in small groups to plan, prepare, or present improvisations as a means of expressing their understanding of a situation, idea, or experience. Small-group work promotes negotiating skills in participants and offers opportunities for exploring characterization, as members devise dialogue and events. Sometimes, groups explore the concepts in the drama, and their discoveries are then used with the whole group in developing a theme. Often, the sharing of group work extends the meaning making of everyone involved in furthering the drama. Groups may also present their work to demonstrate their interpretations of the text being explored.

Guided Tour   Students lead each other on "guided tours" of fictional or real environments. As they guide someone through the space, they share descriptions, offer narration, or answer questions in order to give background and significance to the people who inhabit the space.

Hot-Seating   A student takes on a role and is questioned by the rest of the group. The questioners may speak as themselves or in role. A chair is usually designated as the hot seat — a place for the character in focus to sit and receive questions. Similarly, there may be interviews and interrogations: challenging, demanding situations designed to reveal information, attitudes, motives, aptitudes, and capabilities.

Improvisation   In this type of spontaneous dramatic action, the improvisers are in control of the form, structure, and direction of the drama. Improvisers may be provided with a stimulus, such as specified roles in a specific situation; a problem to solve in a set time; or a challenge that serves as the stimulus for the ensuing dramatic action.

A *prepared* or *polished* improvisation is one that is reworked, reshaped, and rehearsed for sharing or performance; it may be incorporated into the playmaking of the whole group. Rehearsal of lines is usually not part of it.

Inner and Outer Circle   Students gather in two circles usually, with the intention of representing two different characters in the drama. This convention helps students share contrasting perspectives central to a drama. Students in role can describe their reactions and thoughts at a particular point in the drama. Working out of role, they can share personal reflections as they are given prompts. Spontaneous, unrehearsed conversation can be unpacked using this double-circle formation. The outer circle can rotate, and activities can be repeated (sometimes with new prompts) to further experience a variety of points of view or to deepen the learning.

Interviewing   A person or small group, in role of interviewer, asks questions of a student to gain information about an event or a character. Those interviewed can often assume the role of an expert who is able to tell a story or describe or provide facts about a particular situation.

Mantle of the Expert   Students act in role as experts to resolve a problem or challenge. When students wear the Mantle of the Expert, characters have special, specific knowledge that is relevant to the situation or task, gained from previous inquiries or experiences, such as researching a certain time or place. The Mantle of the Expert can empower students and provide them with responsibility, information, and respect.

Masks   The use of masks can develop skills — physical, vocal, communicative, and collaborative — and promote an awareness of how symbolic art forms can be used to affect, communicate with, or manipulate participants or an audience. Masks can lead to an understanding of how our own and other cultures view the world; they can create a character larger than life or be part of a ceremony or ritual.

Meetings   Students and teacher (often in role) come together to hear new information, make decisions, and plan actions or strategies to resolve problems that have emerged in a drama.

Mimed Activity   Mime uses the body to act or interact with something or someone not visible. The use of gesture, movement, and facial expression without words or sounds communicates actions, character, emotions, or relationships. In *occupational mime*, students use their bodies to pretend that they are involved in an occupation.

Narration   A student in or out of role describes the action that is occurring or has occurred in a drama as a reporter, storyteller, witness, or group member.

Objects as Characters   This convention involves fleshing out a character by examining a carefully chosen collection of personal belongings. The objects should provide clues about the character of their owner. Items need to have the potential to raise questions for the group, which tries to interpret them. The group can also be asked to give gifts or talents to a central character within a drama. These gifts can be real artifacts or drawings or writings on paper.

Overheard Conversations/Eavesdropping   Students role-play in small groups, listening in (eavesdropping) on what is being said by different characters in the drama. For this convention, a signal is often given to freeze all the groups, who, in turn, are each "brought to life" to continue improvising while the other groups, as audience, watch and listen. The teacher can also pass by as if he/she is eavesdropping on each scene.

Playmaking   *See* Whole-Group Role Play.

Prepared Role   Another teacher, administrator, parent, classmate, or older student is brought into the drama to play a role accurately and authentically. This person does not come out of role. The teacher facilitates the group's meeting with this role player, someone significant to the developing drama, and involves the group in working with the player.

Questioning   Questions are used by the teacher (and students) both inside and outside drama explorations, both in role and out of role, to give purpose, direction, and shape to the learning activities. Questions can deepen belief and commitment. They can also stimulate the minds of the students to go beyond what they already know.

Readers Theatre   In Readers Theatre, a script is developed from material not initially written for performance. Participants dramatize narration from a text and require opportunities to think about, discuss, and explore the characters whose lines they will interpret. Choral speaking techniques can be incorporated into the presentation. Timing, pacing, and voice can add to the quality of the interpretations.

Ritual   The forms of past rituals offer students involved in drama a way of adding power to their work, focusing the improvised playing with a careful structure that can add solemnity or choreographed movement to the event being explored. Ritual as stylized enactment can move participants more deeply into the drama as they recognize the importance of their actions. Games often retain elements of older rituals.

Role on the Wall   A central role to be explored in the drama is represented in picture form as a diagram or outline on a chart, which is put on the wall. Students reflect on the thoughts, feelings, and qualities that are significant to the character by adding words, statements, or questions around the image. Information about the role is added as the drama is introduced and progresses. This role can be adopted by students in ensuing improvisations.

Role Play   Participants project themselves into a fictitious situation and assume attitudes that are not necessarily their own. These attitudes are usually imposed or suggested by the content or action of the drama, and may be the reverse of their real-life attitudes. The role play develops as the participants solve or work through the dilemma or issue.

Role Reversal   At a significant moment in the drama, students take on roles representing a different status, viewpoint, or occupation than what they had. This convention provides an effective way to examine social interaction, opposing viewpoints, relationships, and motives.

Rumors and Gossip   Students are directed to spontaneously create, spread, and gather rumors about a character or event in the drama. When confined to a designated space, rumors can spread through a hubbub of voices. The teacher can join in and feed the rumors to extend the drama.

Sculpting   One or more students mould others as if they are clay or other sculpting material. This sculpting might involve gentle touching without using any speech, or the sculptor might give verbal instructions to the lump of clay, who responds accordingly. Once the sculpture is completed, audience members can interpret its meaning. Titles can be provided. Perhaps those involved in the sculpture can speak aloud in role. In *group sculpture*, an individual (or members from the group) models volunteers into a shape using as many group members and/or objects as necessary to reflect and encapsulate a particular aspect of the theme or issue under scrutiny. Unlike still image, which tends to favor literal representations, this activity usually produces non-representational images.

Soundscape   Sounds are used to create an atmosphere or to enhance important moments of a scene. Students usually work in groups to agree on and produce the desired sound effects, using voice, recordings and/or instruments, or dialogue, to create a mood, build the atmosphere of a place, or paint a picture with sound. In soundtracking, students use realistic or stylized sounds to accompany an action.

Story Drama   Students are engaged in the dramatic exploration of an idea or event drawn from a story. Rather than being a literal re-enactment of a narrative and its characters, story drama uses the issues, themes, characters, mood, conflict, or spirit of a story as a frame for improvisation. The focus is on an uncertainty, a complex idea, or an event or detail not fully explored within the original story. The term *story drama* has quite different connotations from story enactment or dramatization.

Storytelling   Storytelling includes the retelling of familiar stories as well as the development of new stories. It involves a performer narrating or enacting various roles to bring a story to life. Retelling can provide the initial starting point for a drama. As students retell a text, they can enrich and extend their personal hoard of words, ideas, stories, songs, and concepts, and deepen their understanding and appreciation of literature. Storytelling develops the ability to turn narration into dialogue and dialogue into narration. It provides students with shifting points of view and opportunities to experiment with different styles of language and a variety of voices. It can reveal an unexplained idea in even a well-known story, or it can serve as a way of building reflection in role. Puppetry is one form of storytelling.

Still Image   *See* Tableau.

Tableau   A tableau is also known as a *still image*. Working alone, with a partner, or in small groups, students become motionless figures to represent a scene, theme, important moment(s) in a narrative, or an abstract idea. Important features of a tableau include character, space, gesture, facial expression, and levels. Still images can be shared by one group watching another, or the class can serve as an audience as the work is presented. As tableaux are interpreted, students should be encouraged to consider what messages have been conveyed within a single image.

In *tap and talk*, participants in a still image, freeze frame, or tableau are tapped on the shoulder and then speak aloud a response embedded in the dramatic situation represented. (See also Thought Tracking.)

Taking Sides   Group members place themselves physically on an imaginary line intended to show two positions in a for-or-against debate. Members indicate their preference through their choice of position: the closer someone stands to a given end, the stronger that person's stand on the issue.

Talking Objects   In drama, inanimate objects can speak. The objects might belong to any character or might be part of a setting established by the drama. Students are invited to become objects and tell a little about themselves and the person they belong to; they should also be prepared to answer questions. Alternatively, a talking object could be passed around the circle: a real object is passed from person to person, each having an opportunity to talk as the object.

Teacher as Narrator   Narration can be used to establish mood, to bridge gaps in time, and to register decisions made by the students within the drama. The teacher might provide a narrative link, create atmosphere, offer a commentary, initiate a drama, move the action on, or create tension through narrative.

Teacher as Side-Coach   The teacher gives encouraging or descriptive suggestions as the students act out their ideas in the drama. By suggesting actions and ideas the students might explore, the teacher thereby helps to sustain the drama's momentum. Sometimes, only a few students need side-coaching; sometimes, the whole class requires it. The teacher can point out story ideas or remind the students of ideas mentioned in discussion that could be incorporated. The suggestions should be made tentatively, and the teacher should not try to impose ideas on the group. The teacher can, however, boost confidence in nervous or insecure students or inject enthusiasm into a lacklustre activity through voice. Although side-coaching is normally done by the teacher, occasionally, students may be asked to do it.

Teacher-in-Role When a teacher works in role, she or he adopts a certain set of attitudes to work inside the drama and alongside the students. Acting skill is not required, but the teacher must alter his or her status in the classroom to help students explore issues or examine possible directions that a drama may take. Depending on the role assumed, the teacher can extend the drama, focus attention, challenge the class, suggest alternatives, support contributions, slow the action, and clarify information in order to enhance the commitment, the language, and the thoughts and feelings of the students as they work in a fictional context.

Thought Tracking This convention involves the sharing of the in-role thoughts, questions, or feelings of a character or characters. Most commonly, a signal such as a tap on the shoulder is given for the character to speak a thought out loud.

Whole-Group Role Play All the participants are in role in an imagined setting so that everyone is involved in the drama at the same time and shaping the drama while it is in progress. This strategy, also referred to as *playmaking*, can be very useful when the teacher works from within the action of the developing drama. Students may at times work with partners or in small groups, and their resulting work can be used to build the whole-group drama.

Writing in Role Written messages created in or out of role are a means of reflecting on experience, of introducing a new tension, or of providing evidence; they can also be used as a means of reviewing work or building up a cumulative account of a long sequence of work. Students can write as a given character, adopting the character's voice to express thoughts and feelings about the situation. The writing may take different forms: diary, letter, email, report, text message, review, or contract.

Professional Resources

The titles below represent texts from our drama bookshelf that we encourage you to consider adding to your own bank of professional resources. They reflect our own practice and that of respected peers, and further develop themes raised in this text.

Barrs, Myra, and Valerie Cork. 2001. *The Reader in the Writer*. London: Centre for Literacy in Primary Education.

Baldwin, Patrice, and Mick Waters. 2009. *School Improvement Through Drama*. London: Network Continuum.

Baldwin, Patrice. 2007. *With Drama in Mind*. London: Network Continuum.

Baldwin, Patrice, and Rob John. 2012. *Inspiring Writing Through Drama*. London: Continuum.

Barton, Bob. 2000. *Telling Stories Your Way*. Markham, ON: Pembroke Publishers.

Barton, Bob, and David Booth. 2004. *Poetry Goes to School*. Markham, ON: Pembroke Publishers.

Black, Paul, and Dylan Wiliam. 1990. *Inside the Black Box: Raising Standards Through Classroom Assessment*. London: Department of Education and Professional Studies, Kings College London.

Booth, David. 2005. *Story Drama: Reading, Writing and Role-Playing Across the Curriculum*. Markham, ON: Pembroke.

Booth, David, and Masayuki Hachiya. 2004. *The Arts Go to School*. Markham, ON: Pembroke Publishers.

Bowell, Pam, and Brian S. Heap. 2001. *Planning Process Drama*. London: David Fulton Publishers.

Davis, David, ed. 2010. *Gavin Bolton: The Essential Writings*. England: Trentham Books.

Eisner, Elliott. 2000. *The Arts and the Creation of Mind*. New Haven, CT: Yale University Press.

Flemington, Krista, Linda Hewins, and Una Villiers. 2011. *Journey to Literacy*. Markham, ON: Pembroke Publishers.

Gallagher, Kathleen. 2000. *Drama Education in the Lives of Girls: Imagining Possibilities*. Toronto: University of Toronto Press.

Heathcote, Dorothy. 1984. *Collected Writings on Education and Drama*. Edited by Liz Johnson and Cecily O'Neill. London: Hutchinson.

Lundy, Kathleen Gould. 2008. *Teaching Fairly in an Unfair World*. Markham, ON: Pembroke Publishers.

Mantle of the Expert.com. http:www.mantleoftheexpert.com.

Neelands, Jonathan, and Tony Goode. 2001. *Structuring Drama Work: A Handbook of Available Forms in Theatre and Drama*. Cambridge, UK: Cambridge University Press.

O'Neill, Cecily. 1995. *Drama Worlds: A Framework for Process Drama*. Portsmouth, NH: Heinemann.

Rosenblatt, Louise. 1990. "Retrospect." In *Transactions in Literature*, edited by E.J. Farrell and James Squire. Urbana, IL: National Council of Teachers of English.

Rosenblatt, Louise. 1995. *Literature as Exploration*, rev. ed. New York: Modern Language Association of America.

Royal Shakespeare Company. 2010. *The RSC Shakespeare Toolkit for Teachers*. England: Methuen Drama.

Swartz, Larry. 2002. *The New Dramathemes*, 3d ed. Markham, ON: Pembroke Publishers.

Swartz, Larry, and Debbie Nyman. 2010. *Drama Schemes, Themes, & Dreams*. Markham, ON: Pembroke Publishers.

Wagner, Betty Jane. 1976. *Dorothy Heathcote: Drama as a Learning Medium*. National Education Association.

Wilhelm, Jeffrey. 2002. *Action Strategies for Deepening Comprehension: Using Drama Strategies to Assist Improved Reading Performance*. New York: Scholastic.

Index

Source Acknowledgments for Part B: Demonstrations, Strategies, and Texts for Role-Playing

We are grateful for permission to draw on the following texts.

- "Alone in the Grange" by Gregory Harrison. In *The Night of the Wild Horses* by Gregory Harrison (London: Oxford University Press, 1971).
- *Ann and Seamus* by Kevin Major (Toronto: Groundwood Books/Douglas & McIntyre, 2003).
- *For a Girl Becoming* by Joy Harjo (Tucson: University of Arizona Press, 2009).
- "Francesco de la Vega" by Charles Causley. In *Going to the Fair: Selected Poems for Children* by Charles Causley (London: Puffin/David Hingham Associates, 1996).
- "Happy Endings" by Gail White. In *Disenchantments: An Anthology of Modern Fairy Tale Poetry* edited by Wolfgang Mieder (Hanover, NH: University Press of New England, 1985).
- "He Loved Overripe Fruits" by James Berry. In *A Nest Full of Stars* by James Berry (New York: Greenwillow Books, 2004).
- *Josepha: A Prairie Boy's Story* by Jim McGugan, illustrated by Murray Kimber (Markham, ON: Red Deer Press, 2003).
- *Ludie's Life* by Cynthia Rylant (Orlando: Harcourt, 2006).
- *Silverwing* by Kenneth Oppel (Toronto: HarperCollins Canada, 1997).
- "Some One" by Walter de la Mare. From the estate of Walter de la Mare.
- "Switch on the Night" by Ray Bradbury. In *The Oxford Book of Story Poems* edited by Michael Harrison and Christopher Stuart-Clark (Oxford University Press, 2000).
- "The Bully Asleep" by John Walsh. In *Poets in Hand: A Puffin Quintet* edited by Charles Causley et al. (London: Puffin Books, 1985).
- *The Dust Bowl* by David Booth (Toronto: Kids Can Press, 1999).
- "The Frozen Man" by Kit Wright. In *Rabbiting On* (Lions) by Kit Wright (Waukegan, IL: Fontana Press, 1978).
- "The Honey Gatherer's Three Sons" by William Frederick Padwick Burton. In *The Magic Drum: Tales from Central Africa* by W. F. P. Burton (New York: Criterion, 1962).
- "The Listeners" by Walter de la Mare. From the estate of Walter de la Mare.
- "The Princess" by Sara Henderson Hay. In *Disenchantments: An Anthology of Modern Fairy Tale Poetry* edited by Wolfgang Mieder (Hanover, NH: University Press of New England, 1985).
- "The Reindeer Herder and the Moon" by Bob Barton. In *The Bear Says North: Tales from Northern Lands* by Bob Barton (Toronto: Groundwood, 2003).
- "The Swan Maiden" by Claire Boos. In *Scandinavian Folk and Fairy Tales* edited by Claire Boos (Crown Publishers, 1988).
- *Trouble on the Voyage* by Bob Barton (Toronto: Dundurn Press, 2010).
- "What Has Happened to Lulu?" by Charles Causley. In *Figgie Hobbin: Poems for Children* by Charles Causley (London: Macmillan, 1970/2012).
- "Wouldn't You Like to Know" by Michael Rosen. In *Mind Your Own Business* by Michael Rosen (London: Scholastic, 1996).